Economic Growth and the Environment

Economic Growth and the Environment

On the Measurement of Income and Welfare

Kjell Arne Brekke

Dr Polit in Economics and Senior Research Fellow,
Statistics Norway
and
Affiliate Professor, Department of Mathematics,
University of Oslo, Norway

Edward Elgar
Cheltenham, UK • Lyme, US

Published by
Edward Elgar Publishing Limited
8 Lansdown Place
Cheltenham
Glos GL50 2HU
UK

Edward Elgar Publishing, Inc.
1 Pinnacle Hill Road
Lyme
NH 03768
US

A catalogue record for this book is available from the British Library

Library of Congress Cataloguing-in-Publication Data

Brekke, Kjell Arne.
    Economic growth and the environment : on the measurement of income and welfare / Kjell Arne Brekke.
    Includes bibliographical references.
    1. National income—Environmental aspects—Accounting.
2. Sustainable development—Accounting. 3. Externalities
(Economics)—Accounting. I. Title.
HB141.5.B74 1997
339.3—dc20
                                               96-35152
                                                  CIP

ISBN 1 85898 143 3

Printed and bound in Great Britain by Hartnolls Limited, Bodmin, Cornwall

Contents

List of Figures and Tables

Figures

Tables

Preface

This book originated from a review of the literature on green accounting. It is not a book about green accounting, though, rather it is a study of some questions which were triggered by the study of this literature.

The purpose of the book is first to present an operational method for measuring income in an open economy, but also to point out the limitations of this method. I will also provide a critical review of the measurement of growth in national welfare.

The book is meant to be read from the first to the last chapter. Still, the main part of most chapters, except possibly the last two, can be read independently of the other chapters. For completeness, I have included material that will be well-known to some readers, and hence, I have at ceratain points indicated that some sections could be skipped by those who are already familiar with the material.

I hope that readers with an interest in green accounting and measurement of sustainable development will benefit from reading this book. I have tried to keep the presentation as simple as possible and have assumed only basic knowledge of economic theory. Still, some of the questions discussed are difficult. This is unavoidable, since the measurement of welfare and long-run consumption possibilities touches upon some rather deep questions.

This book would not have been possible without the extensive discussions I have had with many people. Special thanks go to Geir B. Asheim, Richard W. Howarth and Rolf Aaberget for lengthy and very helpful discussions and comments. Thanks also to Knut Alfsen, Karine Nyborg, Iulie Aslaksen, Asbjørn Aaheim, Tore Halvorsen, Kristin Rypdal and Svein Homstvedt, who read and made comments on earlier drafts of parts of this book. Finally, I would like to thank Tone Veiby, who made all the figures for me, and Rune Johansen, who helped me with LaTeX problems. Needless to say, I am solely responsible for any remaining errors.

1. Introduction

In the first half of the nineteenth century, John Stuart Mill claimed that 'it is only in the backwards economies of the world that continued economic growth is still an aim'. In Norway, where I live, the average income has risen to a level about 50 times higher than when Mill made his claim, and continued growth is still a widely accepted political aim.

The aim of continued growth has been subject to discussion, though, especially during the last decades when the consequences of limited reserves of natural resources and environmental degradation have received increasing attention. Not only has the objective been discussed, but also the measurement of growth has been criticized on the grounds that GDP and other national accounting measures do not account for resource extraction and environmental degradation.

Environmental degradation and resource extraction are reasons for serious concern. To take resource scarcity first. The world population has increased from about 1.5 billion in 1900 to currently about 5.6 billion.[1] The industrialized world, with 15 per cent of the population, consumed 52 per cent of the total consumption of primary energy.[2] About 90 per cent of the total commercial energy consumption is based on fossil non-renewable energy sources.[3] Eleven per cent of the earth's fertile soil has been so eroded, chemically altered or physically compacted as to damage its original biotic function.[4]

Such pieces of information are good reasons for concerns about an

---

[1]WCED (1987).
[2]UNDP (1993).
[3]WRI (1986), Table 7.1.
[4]WRI (1994), p. 7.

1

emerging resource scarcity. On the other hand the energy requirement
per unit of GDP has declined by about 10 to 30 per cent from 1970 to
1988, in the OECD countries,[5] and Nordhaus (1992) claims that prices
of natural resources have been declining, an observation that does not
support the view that a resource scarcity is emerging.

Also, when it comes to environmental degradation there are serious
warning signs. From 1750 to 1990 the concentration in the atmosphere
of greenhouse gas CO_2 has increased by 26 per cent (Houghton et al.,
1990). The area of forest is decreasing by about 15.4 million hectares
per year and 4 to 8 per cent of tropical forest species may face extinction
over the next 25 years.[6] In Norway the emissions of nitrogen oxides
have increased by 24 per cent from 1973 to 1992. The emissions of non-
methane volatile organic compounds have increased 53 per cent during
the same period. But here, also, the picture is mixed. The emissions
of nitrogen oxides have been decreasing slightly since 1987, those of
sulphur dioxide have decreased by 76 per cent, and those of lead by 83
per cent during the period from 1973 to 1992.[7]

Resource scarcity and environmental degradation have huge potential impact on human well-being and long-run production possibilities.
To the extent that GDP or other aggregates actually do measure welfare
or income, the treatment of environmental degradation and resource
extraction needs consideration. To take an example: does resource extraction contribute to national income or is it rather depreciation of
natural capital? This type of questions is the starting point for the
discussion in this book, but to evaluate any adjustment in different national accounting aggregates, we first have to make clear precisely what
this aggregate is intended to measure. The suggested adjustments in
the 'Green GDP' literature are usually intended to make more accurate
measurements of income or welfare, but what precisely do we mean by

---

[5]IEA (1987), p. 44.

[6]WRI (1994), p. 7.

[7]Statistics Norway (1995). For data from other countries and a study of the
relationship between growth and pollution, see Grossman (1996).

'income' and 'welfare'?

Even apart from the questions of environmental degradation and re-source extraction, there are good reasons to study the measurement of income and welfare. Do the national accounting measures really mea-sure income or welfare even if we disregard environmental degradation and resource extraction?

The average income in Norway is high both by historical and by world standards. Nevertheless, quite a few Norwegians express dis-satisfaction with their income. Is there something wrong with the in-terpretation of GDP or related aggregates as a measure of income, in addition to the depletion of natural resources?

It is often claimed that GDP is our most important welfare mea-sure, but is it obvious that the general well-being in rich countries is very high? The differences in GDP per capita for different parts of the world are enormous, even if we correct for cost of living. Lucas (1988) claims that the differences are 'too large to be believable'. Sim-ilarly, do GDP differences between the nineteenth century and today, really reflect the true welfare differences? The misery of poverty should not be underestimated, but do the rich achieve so much more of those things that makes a life worth living? In a Norwegian survey where people were asked to name 'what is most important in life', Listhaug and Huseby (1990) found that family relationships came out on top. Family relationships and social networks in general are at most only remotely connected to the level of GDP. To the extent that GDP actu-ally measures welfare it must be in a restrictive sense. Can we define such a narrow welfare concept?

The measurement of income, and especially welfare, has already been much studied. The measurement of welfare touches upon deep problems in the borderline between economics and moral philosophy. In Chapter 5, I review some of these questions, but the main focus will be on an issue that is often neglected in the literature: the measurement of changes in welfare over time. We will also consider the problems of comparing socialwelfare in different countries. These aspects of welfare measurement are especially interesting for the Green GDP discussion, since the main purpose of the GDP measure are measurement of growth or comparison between countries.

1.1   INTERPRETING GDP

Why should we (or should we not) adjust GDP or any other of the current national accounting aggregates? I think the only valid reason for an adjustment is that this makes GDP a better measure of whatever it is intended to measure. While this is a point on which few would disagree, many apparently different arguments for adjusting GDP have been used in the polemics for a Green GDP. In the following I will summarize some of these arguments. A review of what I hold to be invalid reasons for adjustments of GDP, will make the purpose and motivation of the following chapters clearer.

A first argument for adjusting GDP is that resource extraction and environmental degradation are not reflected in current national accounts. As demonstrated above, important changes in the environment and the natural resource base of the world economy are taking place, and there are good reasons to think that these changes have an impact on welfare and income. It is equally clear that these changes are not fully reflected in GDP or any other established measure of income or welfare. Moreover, there are other equally important social and cultural changes that are not reflected either. A few examples from Norway illustrate the changes.[8] From 1960 to 1990, the divorce rate increased by 300 per cent, the reported number of children born outside of marriage increased by 900 per cent, and, at the same time, the share of the population with a close family relationship is stable. From 1981 to 1991 the number of reported serious violent crimes increased by 300 per cent. If we want to adjust GDP to make it a better measure of welfare, should we include these changes?

---

[8]The numbers are from Statistics Norway (1993).

The discussion of what should be included in GDP or similar measures is not new. According to Barber (1967), Adam Smith's use of the term 'wealth' can, with one important qualification, be translated into modern terminology as 'national income'. The important qualification is that Smith restricted the term to the output from 'productive' activities. He thus excluded the activities of 'some of the gravest and most important, and some of the most frivolous professions: churchmen, lawyers, physicians, men of letter of all kind; players, buffoons, musicians, opera-singers, opera-dancers etc' (Barber, 1967, p. 29).

Today these activities are included in the measurement of national income, but still there is controversy on what should be included in a measure of national income. Should we make deductions in national income for resource extraction, environmental degradation, and even for urbanization and increased bureaucracy? Is the current definition of national income better founded than Smith's distinction between productive and non-productive activities?

Another historical example is household production. In the first national account published for Norway, the production in the household sector was included. Aslaksen and Koren (1995) report that, according to Bjerve(former director of Statistics Norway) the important Norwegian economist and Nobel laureate, Ragnar Frisch, held the view that household production should be included in the national accounting. This represents a Scandinavian economic tradition in contrast to the British monetary economic tradition where only productive economic activities yielding monetary flows should be included in GDP. In later national accounts for Norway, household production was excluded to bring the accounts in line with international standards of national accounting.

Why should we include in GDP those sectors that Adam Smith considered non-productive? Should we also include household production, and adjust for resource extraction and environmental degradation? Perhaps we should go even further and adjust the GDP for changes in unemployment, social structure, crime rates and suicide.

That something is not reflected in GDP does not imply that it should be included in some adjusted GDP measure. The changes that have taken place in the last century are much more far-reaching than the GDP measure can possibly reflect. There have been two world wars and many local conflicts. Modern democracy has emerged, women have won the right to vote. Should we count anything that potentially influences individual well-being without being fully reflected in GDP, then the list would be endless. New styles in art and music have emerged, and they can be distributed to a much larger audience than was possible a century ago. The possibility of making films has emerged, and live pictures of news events anywhere in the world can be brought almost instantly into homes via the television. And so forth.

Clearly these changes are important to the everyday life of people and influence welfare. However, they are not fully reflected in GDP measures. We can make an almost endless list of changes that have occurred during the last century, all relevant to the evaluation of welfare, but the main criticism of the GDP measure is that it does not reflect environmental degradation and resource extraction. This must reflect the idea of what something like GDP should measure, and we cannot get to the heart of the discussion without raising the more fundamental questions about what we mean by interpreting national accounting aggregates as measures of income and welfare.

It may be argued that resource extraction and environmental degradation stand out from the other changes that are listed above, since they represent a potentially severe threat to the whole human race. Nevertheless, they are not the only such threat, and even if they were, it would not necessarily imply that they should be included in GDP.

A second argument for adjusting GDP is that such an adjustment is required to give the environment the attention it deserves. As pointed out above, it is widely held that GDP is one of the most important indicators in the national accounts, and clearly as GDP is currently defined it does not account for environmental degradation and resource extraction. At the same time it is also claimed that the problems of environmental degradation and resource extraction receive less attention than they ought to, because they are not accounted for in the national accounting aggregates.

The importance of environmental degradation is an argument for spending resources on providing a solid information foundation for decisions on environmental policy. Disagreement on whether or how to make a Green GDP should not be interpreted as disagreement over the importance of sound information on environmental issues. It is not obvious that most useful information is provided by including environmental concerns in GDP. Nor is it clear that environmental issues will receive more attention by making an adjustment to GDP.

To take an example: unemployment has consequences for social welfare. It is a waste of resources when people who are willing to work are unemployed. Those who are unemployed often feel useless and suffer a loss of self-respect. This may then lead to other social problems, such as suicide and increasing crime rates. Even for those who are not unemployed, the possibility of becoming unemployed is a source of uncertainty which will influence their well-being. While all these consequences of unemployment are important to welfare, only the production that is lost by having people idle, is reflected in GDP. Perhaps the most important welfare consequences of unemployment are thus excluded. However, low unemployment is an important aim for most governments.

Of course we do not lack indicators of unemployment, but the welfare consequences of unemployment are not included in GDP. My own casual investigations indicate that most Norwegians have better knowledge about the unemployment rate than about the GDP growth rate. It is not obvious that unemployment would receive more attention if the welfare consequences of unemployment were included in the GDP measure. Nor is it clear that a welfare measure that included the welfare consequences of unemployment would be more useful than current GDP. Decision makers may become suspicious about how production and unemployment are aggregated, and would probably prefer to have separate measures for each of them.

I will argue that a similar argument applies to resource extraction and environmental degradation. Even though environmental degradation is much more complex than unemployment, and cannot be represented by one single number, physical indicators may be more informative and give environmental issues more attention than they would get merely by including them in GDP. This does not rule out including effects of environmental degradation in the GDP or another aggregate, provided this improves the aggregate as a measure of whatever it is intended to measure.

Even if it were true that environmental issues would receive more attention if they were included in the system of national accounts, inclusion should not be chosen purely for a tactical reason. We may change measures such as GDP if this makes them more informative, but the measures should not be chosen to manipulate decision makers. To correct GDP we have to start with the question: what do we want to measure? The literature basically considers two different answers: income and welfare.

Postel (1990) argues that 'To enter the future with economic indicators that ignore the environment is like steering an aircraft toward a fog-shrouded runway without instruments to guide the landing'. But we cannot – only from these observations – conclude that alternative GDP figures which take environmental damage into account should be calculated. To use Postel's methaphor: to adjust GDP for environmental degradation may be to steer an aircraft towards a fog-shrouded runway with only one instrument to guide the landing. Instead of trying to correct the measurement of height, for example, for wind, speed and position, a separate measure for each one of these factors is definitely preferable. It may similarly be preferable to have separate indicators for national income and the state of the environment. *Aggregated information is useful only if it can be clearly interpreted.*

This book is inspired by the discussion of 'greening' the GDP, but it is not a book on national accounting. The focus is rather on the interpretation of aggregated information. What does a national income measure tell us? What is national welfare? And how should environmental degradation and resource extraction influence their measurement?

1.2 MEASURING INCOME

To improve the income measures, we first have to define income. There seems to be a consensus in the literature that the best definition is due to Hicks's (1946) formulations that national income is the amount a nation can spend without impoverishing itself. In Hicks (1946), the famous definition of income is followed by a critical discussion of its shortcomings. He concluded that income is a useful concept for practical purposes, but not for theoretical investigations.

In Chapter 3 we will discuss how this definition can be operationalized for an individual country. We will assume that the country is a small open economy. Income will, in line with Hicks's definition, be defined as maximum sustainable consumption. I will argue that if the interest rate and population are constant, income is the return to wealth. I will also demonstrate how to correct for changes in interest rates and population growth. In particular, we will see that constant wealth is not sufficient for sustainability in these cases. Unlike many of the proposals in the literature, the income from resource extraction will be neither zero nor a share of current resource rent.[9] I will demonstrate that income from resource extraction may even exceed current rent.

The income estimates presented in Chapter 3 consider only the commercial value of resources, while a potential resource scarcity will be given as an exogenous fact, represented by increasing prices on resources. With all prices given, the measurement of income is reduced to determining the intertemporal budget set. The estimated income will

---

[9]The resource rent comprises revenues from resource extraction which exceed what would have been earned in an alternative activity and with the same use of input factors. See Chapter 3.

be very sensitive to various assumptions about the future, especially prices and interest rates. We will see that the presence of uncertainty poses both conceptual and practical problems.

In Chapter 4, we consider the case of a closed economy. This allows us to endogenize the problem of potential resource scarcity. The central question in this chapter is to determine whether the closed economy impoverishes itself, and to consider the consistency of the income measurement from different open economies. If no open economy is using more than their income, is the world economy then sustainable?

1.3   MEASURING WELFARE

Daly and Cobb (1989, Chapter 3) argue that 'All groups assume that GNP measures something of importance to the economy, and most assume that it is closely bound up with human welfare'. The welfare interpretation of GDP is probably the one that is most invoked in arguments for adjustment to GDP. At the same time, when we turn to welfare measures we find the largest variety of proposals and the least consensus.

It is beyond the scope of this book to more than sketch the different issues involved in the measurement of welfare. The discussion will rather focus on issues related to the measurement of economic growth and the environment. We cannot measure social welfare if it is a subjective quantity, and therefore I will focus especially on the uniqueness of social welfare. I will argue that social welfare represents a ranking of social states, and that the ranking depends on whose judgement it is based on. This introduces a subjectivity, due among other things, to the lack of an objective basis for an interpersonal comparison of well-being. If so, welfare is not a unique quantity to be measured.

From the growth and sustainability perspective, a crucial question is how can we compare social welfare at different points in time or in different countries? Economic welfare theory is based on the idea of revealing preferences from choices, but in principle there are no choices that I can make to reveal whether I am better off today than I was yesterday. If preferences are constant over time, there may be a practical solution to this problem, but I will argue that there are well-established individual and social mechanisms which make preferences change over time, and that these changes are to some extent predictable.

As we argued above, many changes that have taken place during the last decades are important to individual well-being, but are not reflected in GDP. The focus primarily on environmental issues indicates that welfare is interpreted in a restricted sense. Many of the proposed adjustments of GDP are intended to improve the measurement, not of welfare, but of economic welfare – but what is 'economic' welfare? A possible answer, to be considered in Chapters 5 and 6, is that economic welfare is a measure of the economic resources that are supposed to be important to achieve welfare.

In Chapter 6 I discuss some of the adjustments that have been suggested to measure the welfare consequences of environmental degradation. With some of these there are serious problems in comparing welfare in different years or in different countries. I will also argue that many of these proposals are actually measures of income, given some restrictions on environmental degradation.

1.4   THE INTERCONNECTION BETWEEN ECONOMY AND ENVIRONMENT

This book is not about national accounting; however the national accounting aggregates are the best-known measures of either national income or welfare, and hence much of the discussion will relate to them. It is thus natural to start with a sketch of the System of National Accounts (SNA) 1993. This is the purpose of the next chapter. We also discuss some of the other national aims of accounting, not related to measurement of income or welfare.

In this book I will be rather sceptical of many of the proposals for a greener GDP, especially those that are intended to measure welfare. This scepticism should not be interpreted as a claim that resource extraction and environmental degradation are not areas for serious concern. The discussion here is about how to present the relevant information. It is because this information is important that we have to take this subject seriously.

It is important that we are able to see the consequences of economic growth and economic policy on the environment. For this we not only need accounting, that is, measure what has happened in the past, but we must also be able to analyse the consequences of alternatives that are not yet implemented. Such analysis requires models, and modelling requires data. National accounting data have been essential to the construction of models of national economies, and if we want to extend these models to include environment and natural resources, resource accounts and environmental statistics must be consistent with the SNA conventions.

2. National Accounting, Environment and Resources

A discussion of the measurement of national income and welfare cannot possibly ignore the national accounts. Among the aggregates in the national accounts are the current measures that are most used or interpreted as measures of income or welfare. The central national accounting measures such as gross domestic product (GDP) and net national income (NNI), have undoubtedly become very important in how we perceive the performance of a national economy. GDP growth is an important political aim, and we divide the world into rich and poor countries according to their per capita GDP.

The rules for the compilation of the national accounts are given in the System of National Accounts (SNA). The System of National Accounts, is, as the name indicates a *system*, and not just a mere description of a set of economic indicators. Frisch (1939) stated in his definition of national accounting that it is crucial that national accounting data are 'presented in a way that allows the interrelationships between different data to be clearly demonstrated'. A new definition for one part of the system, requires a revision of the whole system. An important challenge to any attempts to improve the main measures, such as GDP, is thus to incorporate these improved measures into a consistent accounting system.

The focus of this book is the measurement of income and welfare, not an examination of the total national accounting system. To the extent that national accounting issues are discussed it will be restricted

13

to comments on the main measures such as GDP and NNI, as measures of income and welfare. The remaining parts of the system will not be considered. This is not a denial of the importance of the consistency of the accounting system, but the implementation of any proposal considered may require an adjustment of the complete system, which would be beyond the scope of this book.

2.1   A BRIEF INTRODUCTION TO NATIONAL ACCOUNTING

In this section I will give a very short description of the main national accounting concepts, and their current definition. This section is actually an introduction only to the main SNA quantities, and not to the accounting *system*. Those who are familiar with the System of National Accounts (SNA) could skip this section, and proceed directly to Section 2.2. For those who want more information on national accounting, see Ruggles (1987) or for a more extensive description, see System of National Accounts (1993).

The SNA has been revised several times, and the last version is the SNA 1993. The alternative versions of SNA differ with respect to both the definition and the names of the aggregates. In SNA 1993, GNP and NNP are renamed, respectively, gross national income, GNI, and net national income, NNI. The term 'gross domestic product, GDP', is left unaltered. In the remainder of the book, I will consistently use the SNA 1993 concepts, except in some quotations.

The gross domestic product, GDP, measures the total output produced in an economy during a year. Total output is a mixture of goods such as apples, tyres and books, along with services such as dental care and haircuts. To combine these heterogeneous goods and services, GDP measures the *value* of total output, where each good and service is valued at market prices.

Valuation at market prices is not uniformly applied, because some goods and services have no market prices, such as the services from governmental bureaucracy or the police force. Governmental services are valued at cost, thus wages of government employees are their contribution to GDP. Similarly, for most goods produced in households, there are no market prices, and the value of this output is generally not included in GDP, except for part of the household production in farm households.

To avoid double counting, only the value of *final* output is included in GDP. For example, GDP will not include both the value of a piece of clothing, and the value of fabrics sold to the manufacturer of the clothes. The goods used as input in production are termed *intermediate* goods. In practice, double counting is avoided by working with *value added*. Thus the contribution to GDP from the manufacturer is the value of clothes produced, minus the value of the intermediate goods used as input in production. Furthermore, GDP measures only the value of currently-produced output; transactions of existing commodities, such as old cars or existing houses, are not included in GDP.

A closely related concept is gross national income, GNI. The difference between GDP and GNI is that GDP is a measure of what is produced within the economy, while GNI is the income that is earned by citizens of the nation either as compensation to employees or as property income. To derive GNI from GDP we would have to extract compensation to foreign citizens within the economy and add the compensation received by national citizens as employees in foreign economies. Similarly property income earned by foreigners within the economy should be subtracted, and property income earned by national citizens outside the nation should be added.

Net national income, NNI, (similar to the net national product, NNP) is derived from GNI by deducting the depreciation of existing capital during the period. Machines wear out as they are used and buildings depreciate over time. The idea is that unless worn-out machines are replaced and buildings are properly maintained, production cannot be kept at the current level over a longer period of time. This idea is similar to the idea behind the Hicksian definition of income, to be discussed later.

2.1.1   Real and Nominal Measures

To compare numbers from different years, we should use *real* measures. Real GDP values the output at two points in time *at the same prices,* while nominal GDP values the output during a year at current prices: the market prices of that year. By valuing all goods at constant prices, real GDP is an attempt to measure the physical changes in output. If the output of all commodities were equal in two consecutive years, but prices increased, nominal GDP would increase while real GDP would be constant. In this book we will refer only to real measures, unless otherwise stated. Thus GDP growth, for example, is taken to mean growth in real GDP.

Real GDP is a quantity measure in the sense that only quantity changes matter and not price changes. If the value of real estate is increasing, this would not influence real GDP, which is measured from prices in a base year. On the other hand, if more is produced of each commodity, then GDP will increase. That GDP is a quantity measure should, however, not be taken too literally.

To illustrate, consider Daly's (1991) suggestion that a distinction should be made between growth and development. While he defines 'development' as pursuing the ultimate ends of the population, he defines 'growth' as increasing the 'physical size of the economy', an expression which is intended to represent the economy's pressure on the environment.

GDP is a quantity measure, but it is not a measure of the physical size of the economy. It is not especially clear how the physical size of the economy might be construed, but the idea is that if more natural resources are required as inputs to production and if more waste is generated, then the physical size has increased. GDP includes the value of goods and services with very different requirement of resource input, in production, and since the composition of GDP may change over time, GDP may increase without increasing the physical size of the economy.

To take the extreme case, suppose that output of services such as courses in self-improvement or even an ascetic life style, increase sharply, while the output from industrial sectors is decreasing and where the relative strength of the different shifts is such that real GDP increases. Whatever the precise meaning of 'the physical size of the economy' is taken to be, it has hardly increased in this scenario. On the other hand, with a fixed composition of commodities, GDP growth implies increasing resource use.

2.2   THEORY AND MEASUREMENT

Green GDP measures are mostly meant to measure the performance of the economy either in the form of income or of welfare, but measurement of income and welfare is not the only purpose of the national accounts. SNA (1993) states that SNA is

> a multi-purpose system designed to meet the requirements of different kinds of users: governments, businesses, research institutes, universities, the press and the general public. No single user, or group of users, can take priority over all others. ... to gauge changes in welfare may be one important use of the System, but it is only one use. (paragraph 1.82)

A redefinition of GDP to better meet one purpose, may make it less useful for other purposes. These conflicts were well known to the national accounting pioneers. Ohlsson (1953) argued that different accounting systems should be developed for different purposes. His suggestion was not listened to, and instead, GDP was developed as a compromise between the requirements from conflicting objectives, see Aukrust (1994). The advantage of this approach is obvious, since only one system is needed. On the other hand, the resulting estimates are not the best possible for each purpose. It should be noted, though, that recently the concept of 'satellite accounts' has been developed to tailor the account for special purposes, such as accounting for household production or resource extraction and environmental degradation. A satellite account is separate from, but consistent with, the national account.

To illustrate the consequences of having one account to serve multiple purposes, it is illuminating to consider the contrast between the use of GDP in Keynesian models and the measurement of welfare or some related concept. This also illustrates some important points on the connection between theory and measurement. We start with a Keynesian model.

Total production in an economy is a key variable of different economic models, from neoclassical growth models to Keynesian short-term models. These different models are designed to analyse very different problems. Keynes's main objective was to explain unemployment, while growth models are intended to analyse long-run development in productive capacity and typically assume that the labour market is in equilibrium. Since the purpose of these models is different, the ideal measurement of total production may be different.

Consider a simple Keynesian multiplier model. Let C, I, Y and L be positive real numbers, and suppose that

$$C = c(Y)$$
$$Y = C + I$$
$$Y = f(L)$$

where $c(Y)$ and $f(L)$ are positive continuous increasing functions and where c satisfies $c(Y) < Y$.

As stated this is a mathematical structure, defining a relationship between some real numbers. Provided $c(Y) < Y - I$ for Y sufficiently large, the structure defines C and Y as functions of I, and then L is determined by Y. To make this a model of the real world, we would have to specify what quantities in the real world correspond to C, I, Y and L. We can easily turn the model into nonsense, for example, by letting C denote the temperature in Oslo in June, while Y is GDP. For the multiplier model to be a reasonable model, the description of the real-world objects corresponding to each of the variables is essential.

Some indications of the corresponding real-world objects are given by reading the numbers as 'consumption', 'investment', 'total production', and 'labour demand', respectively. However, this still gives only a vague indication, since there are many different potential definitions and methods of measurement for these quantities. To make this a model of the real world, we would have to specify further, for example, by defining C as total (private and governmental) consumption, measured according to SNA 1993. Now the SNA becomes an essential part of the model specification.

But this use of the SNA has implications for how the quantities in SNA are measured. Within the Keynesian framework the logic is that as the national product increases, more labour input is required, and hence unemployment will decrease. This is based on the assumption that production is limited from the demand side. To be useful within this tradition, measures of national product should not include output which does not require labour input.

To illustrate this point, consider the case of household production which was included in the first Norwegian national account, but is excluded from the main account in the current SNA. Increased household production is not likely to cause increased labour demand, at least not on the formal labour market. Including household production in the measurement of Y, we would have to include the labour input in household production as part of the labour demand. In the next instance we would have to take into account the labour use in household production in the definition of unemployment. Thus the mapping between the variable Y and the real-world observations are essential to what problems the model can be used to study.

A similar argument indicates that it would not be reasonable to include services from the environment in total production in the Keynesian model. It is hardly possible to redefine L so that the last equation is reasonable if environmental services are included in Y.

From the perspective of neoclassical growth theory, the focus is very different. Unemployment is usually disregarded altogether, and the perspective is moved to how much the economy produces. It is irrelevant whether this is produced within the formal economy. From this perspective, household production is highly relevant.

A simple static model can illustrate this. Consider the mathematical structure with the real numbers, U and Y, the non-negative vectors, p and x, and a function, u. The mathematical structure is

$$U = \max_z u(z) \text{ subject to } pz \leq Y.$$

Once again this is only a mathematical structure, with no economic content until the corresponding real-world objects are defined. The structure defines U as a function of p and Y, as indicated by the function, v. We give the symbols names that indicate the corresponding real-world object, as when we read U as 'instantaneous utility' or 'welfare', and the vector, x, is read as 'consumption bundle' and Y as the 'income' or 'current expenditure on non-capital goods'. As above, we need to specify the measurement of these quantities to make it a model of the real world. An additional problem is that there are no well-defined observable real-world objects which correspond to U, and so we are usually left only with the indication given by naming it 'welfare'.

While welfare U is unobservable, it is an increasing function of income Y. For example, if Y is national income as measured in the national account, welfare is linked to some observable quantity. To make this link reasonable, a definition of Y is required, which is different from that of the Keynesian model. Now it will be reasonable to include household production among the goods and services included in z. Should we also include environmental services? Can we extend the structure $pz \leq Y$ to such services? We return to these questions in Chapters 5 and 6.

These two examples illustrate the importance of being explicit about the mapping between variables in theoretical models and real-world objects. This question is studied at length in Stigum (1990). In this book we consider the measurement of income and welfare, that makes the 'neoclassical perspective' the most relevant. This is the perspective we take when we divide the world into rich and poor countries according to per capita GDP. From this perspective, GDP is taken as a measure of national welfare. But to discuss what is the best measure of national welfare we first need to define the entity we want to measure, that is, what exactly is 'national welfare'? A similar comment applies to the evaluation of net national income. What exactly do we mean by 'national income'?

The discussion above illustrates that to answer these questions we have to specify the theoretical model, and the real-world objects which correspond to the variables in the model. The discussion above also illustrate that it is the questions we want to analyse with the model which are important. The exclusion of services from the environment in the definition of Y in the Keynesian model, was because the intended use of the model was to explain labour demand. Similarly the appropriate measure of income or welfare depends on the purpose of measuring income or welfare. On the importance of the purpose of measurement, see also Aaheim and Nyborg (1995).

2.3   RESOURCE AND ENVIRONMENTAL ACCOUNTS

As pointed out above, the SNA is an accounting *system*. Producing aggregate measures is only one of the reasons for having national accounts. An equally important purpose is to clarify the interdependencies between different parts of the economy. How much of the production is used, for example, for private consumption, for investment, or for military expenditures?

Extending this kind of information to natural resources and environmental quality would mean compiling information for example on emissions to air which are made by the economic sector. Such extensions can be made without measuring the environment in monetary terms or changing the aggregates. The natural resource accounting in Norway is an early attempt in this direction. It provides information on the use of different resources, by sector, plus an account of the stock and changes in stocks. Similarly it provides information on what quantities of different pollutants are emitted to the air, and by which sector. The accounts are in physical units, and do not influence the national accounting aggregates. Much of the criticism of the national accounts for misrepresenting the dependencies of natural resources and the environment, derives from to the lack of information on the interrelations between the economy and the environment. Even though these interrelations do not directly concern the measurement of income and welfare, they have a bearing on the relationship between economic growth and the environment, and it is natural to include some comments on this issue.

In Norway the development of a natural resource accounting system was initiated in the early seventies. Førsund and Strøm (1976) extended input–output tables by estimating emissions to air, land and water of different pollutants, classified according to consumption, export, investment or production categories. See also Førsund (1985). Later, a natural resource accounting system was established on a regular basis. Among the criteria which were considered for this development was:

> The definitions of sectors and commodities in the resource account should, if possible, follow the definitions of the National Accounts. While the National Accounts are kept in monetary units, the resource accounts are kept in physical units. By combining the two, it is possible to obtain price indices for many of the natural resources, and to link resource use to economic activity. (Alfsen et al. 1986, p. 15)

In the initial phase of resource accounting in Norway, accounts kept of energy, fish and land use. In addition less detailed accounts were kept of minerals, forests and sand and gravel. Later, inventories of emissions to air were established. The accounts are in physical units and consist of three sub-accounts covering: reserves; extraction, transformation and trade; and national use of the resources

Note that not only the reserves, but also the flows are accounted for. Both the last two accounts are by economic sector. The account on extraction, transformation and trade covers extracting, production, the use of energy as intermediate input in the energy sectors, and the foreign trade of energy. This determines how much is available for use in the remaining economy. Finally, the accounts show the use of energy by sector in the rest of the economy. The system has been extended to give the emissions to air by sector.

Integrating information on economic activity, resource use and the environment into a consistent framework will be useful, no matter how resource use and environmental degradation are taken into account in measures of income or welfare. Work on developing such information systems is going on in many different countries and organization, for example, the NAMIA in the Netherlands (Keuning, 1993).

Connecting this information to models of the economy, we may project the use of energy and emissions to air along the expected economic development, and see how the energy use and emissions will respond to different economic instruments. This is the topic of the next section.

2.4   MODELS OF THE ENVIRONMENT AND THE ECONOMY

Information about which sectors are emitting a particular pollutant is important in understanding the source of the problem, and in designing policies to reduce the emission of that pollutant. On the other hand, the studies do not indicate the effect of different policy instruments. For example, they show which sectors are emitting CO_2, but not what the effect of increasing the carbon tax would be. To get an impression of this effect, we would need a model of the economy and its relation to the environment.

In the last decade, many economic models have been developed which aim at integrating linkages to the environment. Global models include Edmunds and Reilly (1983), Manne and Richels (1990) and Rutherford (1992). Models for smaller regions include Jorgensson and Wilcoxen (1993), Bergman (1990) and Conrad and Schröeder (1990). It is beyond the scope of this book to give a survey of such models, but some of the Norwegian experiences with this kind of work are highly relevant.

In Norway, the development of such models has been dependent upon the natural resource accounts. Just as the national accounts provide essential data for estimating models of the national economy, the natural resource accounts provide essential data when these models are to be extended to include the environment and natural resource use. The resource accounts give information on current and past interconnection between resource use, the environment and economic activities, but this is not sufficient for analyses of the consequences of alternative policies.

The first macroeconomic study of this kind in Norway was done in 1988. In this study a macroeconomic model was used to forecast future CO_2-emissions under different policies (Bye et al., 1989). Many studies has followed[1]. Most of these studies are based on the general equilibrium model.

One of the arguments that has been used for correcting the GDP is that it would give environmental issues the weight they deserve. But a Green GDP is not only way of showing how environmental issues are related to economic policy. I think that the experiences from Norway show that macroeconomic models with linkages to the environment are better suited for this purpose. To what extent the model-based analyses have actually influenced policy is hard to evaluate, but we can trace

---

[1]Later studies include Moum (ed.) (1992), and Glomsrød et al. (1992).

some effects on the process of developing the long-term economic policy. An example is the government's 'Long-term Programme 1994–97'.

The Long-term Programme (LTP) states the main future prospects as the government sees them, and the plans for the long-term policy. While the economy is only one part of the problem area, it is a crucial one, since it will determine the resources available for different purposes, and the Ministry of Finance has the responsibility for coordinating its work with the LTP. The economic perspectives presented in the LTP are based on simulations of a general equilibrium model, MSG which has also been used with study the linkages to the environment.

Since models of emissions to air are integrated into this model, the simulation would easily provide a perspective, not only on economic development, but also on emissions. Moreover, if the Ministry of Finance does not compute the emissions forecast which follows from their economic forecasts, then others will do. As a consequence, the LTP 1994–97 for the first time presented such perspectives, consistent with the economic perspectives presented.

There are currently many proposals for developing a green GDP, but little consensus. In the following chapters I will be rather sceptical of many of the proposed adjustments, especially the attempts to measure welfare. Given this lack of consensus, it is important to stress the areas where there appears to be much more agreement. While we may disagree on how to measure welfare or income, I think there would be much more agreement on the need to compile information on the interconnections between the economy and the environment and to incorporate environmental issues into economic models.

3. Income in Open Economies

In many countries revenues from natural resource extraction comprise a considerable share of GDP. But are their revenues from resource extraction really income or just depreciation of natural capital? What is the correct income in those countries? For extraction of non-renewable resources the similarity with depreciation of capital is particularly clear, since the reserves must be declining, but for all resources the creation of revenues may be accompanied by changes in stock. We need a method to deal with all kinds of income from resource-based production, from extraction of exhaustible resources, to fisheries to agricultural revenues in countries with extensive soil degradation.

We start the investigation of this question with an analysis of resource extraction in a small open economy, where all prices are determined abroad. This simplifies the analysis considerably, since we do not have to keep track of the general equilibrium consequences of the extraction policy. On the other hand, the open economy model leaves out crucial questions about extraction of resources. If an oil exporting country has exhausted its reserves of oil, it can import oil from abroad, assuming the resource has not been completely extracted on a global level, but if all countries have extracted their resources, the resource will not be available on the world market. This would require a global study of resource extractions, which is left for the next chapter.

In this and the next chapter we consider only the commercial value of natural resources. Clearly, natural resources such as forests and fish-stocks are important not only because of the market value of timber and fish, but also because of the more direct effect on human well-being, for example, by providing recreational services. I leave those aspects of resource extraction for later chapters. The restriction to market value allows us to use Hicks's definition of income with its straightforward interpretation, without having to face the problem of defining welfare.

3.1 HICKSIAN INCOME

The purpose of income calculation in practical affairs is to give people an amount they can consume without impoverishing themselves. Following out that idea, it would seem that we ought to define a man's income as the maximum value that he can consume during a week, and still expect to be as well off at the end of the week as he was in the beginning (Hicks, 1946, Chapter 14, p. 172)

This well-known passage from Hicks has become the standard definition of income. Hicks proceeds to discuss this definition with the help of a specific example, starting with the suggestion that a nation is 'equally well off' at the end of the year as in the beginning if its wealth is equally high at the end of the year. After a discussion of several problems with this definition, he concludes that the income concept was unsuitable for theoretical analysis, but interesting from a practical point of view.

We will return to Hicks's discussion below, but first note that the term 'equally well off' in the definition, can be interpreted in terms of both affluence and welfare. In this chapter, we consider only the affluence interpretation, which is the one that Hicks used in the discussion following the definition.

The amount a person chooses to spend during a week determines his/her budget set for the week. Any consumption vector that costs less than the chosen expenditure is then feasible. With fixed prices, his/her income fully determines the choice set. In spite of the enormous variety in different commodities that can be bought and sold, the one number completely characterizes the set of feasible consumption vectors. A simple interpretation of 'as well off' is that the budget set in future years is at least as large as in the current year.

Consider the management of financial wealth, and suppose that relative prices and the interest rate are constant over time. If the wealth is non-decreasing, any consumption path that is available at time t is also available at time $s > t$. We do not have to consider the welfare the person is able to achieve from the set of allowable consumption paths, we note only that future budget sets are at least as large as the current one. The budget sets are ranked according to set-inclusion, and no reference to welfare is needed.

In this simple model it is possible to keep a sharp distinction between income and the welfare achieved from income. This distinction will be a central one in this book. Unfortunately, it is not possible to keep the distinction equally clear when more realistic assumptions are introduced. The simple model above relies on the assumption that relative prices and real interest are constant. Some examples illustrate the importance of these very restrictive assumptions.

First consider the case of a variable interest rate. Suppose that the wealth is $100,000 and the interest rate is 10 per cent, then the return on the wealth is $10,000. If the interest rate the next year falls to 5 per cent, then the return on the wealth would fall to $5,000, and the person would not be equally well off at the end of the year. Equally well off should thus not be taken to mean constant wealth. The wealth itself is just an accounting identity – the monetary value of the asset holding. To be equally well off, the person should be able to maintain his/her consumption expenditures. Still wealth is important; when future interest rates are known, the wealth is sufficient to determine the future consumption possibilities.

Suppose that the fall in interest rate from 10 per cent to 5 per cent was known in advance. It would then be easy to correct for this fall. If the person spends approximately $5,238 and saves the remaining $4,762, the wealth would increase to $104,762. The return on this higher wealth at 5 per cent interest rate would be about $5,238.

Thus, spending $5,238 is sustainable in the long run. Note that in this case, spending no more than the Hicksian income would imply that the wealth should strictly be increasing. Nevertheless, we can keep a clear distinction between income and welfare.

The second problem pointed out by Hicks is price changes. The easy case is when the price level changes, but relative prices are constant. To cope with such shifts in the price level, we have to do the calculation in real prices, with real interest rates. The problem arises when relative prices change. Hicks could point to no completely satisfactory solution to changes in relative prices, and concluded that the income concept was useful for practical purposes, but not for theory building. Nevertheless, we should search for a good definition of income 'for practical purposes'.

It is sufficient to consider the case of two commodities to see the kind of problems that arise if relative prices change. This situation is illustrated in Figure 3.1. The two budget sets represented by the budget lines a and b cannot be ranked by set-inclusion. It is possible to rank the sets according to preferences. If x_a is the best choice from the budget set a, and x_b is the best choice from b, we would prefer the budget set a to b if we prefer x_a to x_b. Thus, we may claim that the budget set a corresponds to a higher income than in b, since more welfare is achieved in a than in b. But this definition of income would make the distinction between income and welfare less clear.

Do nations really choose from the national budget set to maximize some social welfare function, as indicated in Figure 3.1? We observe that nations with similar economic resources can spend their income very differently. Even the preferred economic policy of different groups within the same country may be very different.

This is very important for practical purposes, for example, Drèze and Sen (1989) point out that even poor countries can afford quite extensive health care and education. In poor countries wages are low and since health care and education is labour intensive, health care is much cheaper in a poor country than in a rich one. This illustrates the problem with differences in relative prices.

Figure 3.1 Using preferences to rank budget sets

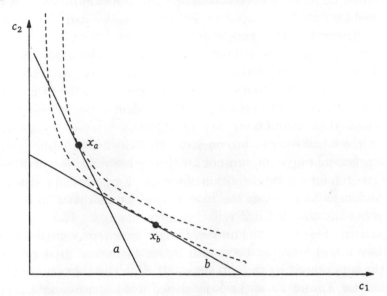

The well-being of the population depends upon how the economic resources are used. While some very poor countries do provide extensive health care, there are much richer countries which do not. In the yearly Human Development Report from UNDP, development is seen as reflected by indicators such as high literacy rate, long life expectancy and low child mortality, which are correlated to income, but not perfectly. For example, UNDP (1993, Figure 1.5) shows countries where 'development is ahead of income', that is, countries with high literacy rate, long life expectancy and low child mortality, in spite of low income. Political systems, institutions and culture are important in this respect.

In order to talk about nations that have succeeded in developing in spite of a low income, we should rank budget set not only according to the preferences over the chosen consumption vector, but rather we should think of the budget set as reflecting the economic resources of the nation. Whether the nation manages to use these resources wisely, is a separate question.

The problem with this approach is that we would need some kind of ranking of budget sets. Sen (1991) considers ranking of chosen sets as indexes of the freedom of choice for a single individual. He concludes that a ranking only on the basis of preferences over the preferred choice is too narrow, but that any reasonable measure of the freedom of choice has to be related to preferences.

Not only is it difficult to base a comparison between countries on preferences, but also a comparison of different years for the same country gives rise to some theoretical difficulties. It is not obvious that the consumption in different years has independent utility. We will discuss this problem at length in Chapter 5.

It would be nice to distinguish economic resources from achievements. However, we have to cope with changes in relative prices, and then we cannot completely discard preferences. The solution chosen in the national accounts is to use price indexes. This implies ranking budget sets according to the best alternative, so that a would be preferred to b in Figure 3.1 (see also Diewert, 1987). The previous discussion should then be read as a warning that different relative prices are a problem in the use of income estimates for two countries to as a basis for comparison of either economic resources or actual achievements.

3.2   THE CAKE-EATING ECONOMY

The Hicksian definition of income is especially interesting for the estimation of income from resource extraction. Extraction non-renewable resources implies that the remaining stock is reduced. If we think of resources as natural capital, we may ask whether a nation can be as well off at the end of the year without somehow compensating for this reduction. To illustrate the problem, consider the rather drastic case of a 'cake-eating' economy.

A 'cake-eating economy' is an economy that is living purely on one resource stock. Every unit of consumption reduces the stock of this resource by one unit and when there are no more resources left, no more consumption is possible. With an infinite horizon, the Hicksian income in this economy is clearly zero, since with any consumption level, however small, the economy will eventually run out of resources and the consumption be zero.

This argument presumes that the economy has an infinite horizon. If we require only that the consumption should be sustainable within a finite horizon, a positive consumption is possible, but it may be very small. With a very long horizon, for example, until the sun burns up, the allowable consumption will be very low indeed.

If the economy is a small part of a larger world economy, the situation may become very different, especially if we assume that the nation can save money in foreign bonds with a certain rate of return, and that this return is constant over time, and moreover that world market prices are constant. In this case the country can sell its entire resource stock – the cake – and place the money in bonds. The return from this financial wealth is an infinite income stream, and since world market prices are assumed to be constant, it is possible to use this income to spend a constant amount on consumption goods from abroad. Thus the same resource can in this case support an infinite positive consumption stream.

Thus, opening up the economy completely alters the conclusion. This is no paradox. By assuming constant prices and constant interest rates we have in fact assumed that the total world economy is no cake-eating economy. The opportunity to trade on the world market changes the technology of the nation from a cake-eating technology to one where capital gives a positive return for ever.

If the world as a whole is cake-eating, no part of it can sustain a positive consumption level for ever. A cake-eating world economy is thus inconsistent with the assumption that prices and interest rates are constant.

3.3 HICKSIAN RESOURCE INCOME IN THE OPEN ECONOMY

How do we calculate the Hicksian income from resource extraction, in a small open economy? In the following we will demonstrate how this income can be found by computing the resource wealth, defined as the present value of resource rent.

There is in principle no reason to restrict the attention to the income from resource extraction. The same argument would apply to all components of national income. Resource extraction is, however, particularly important for the discussion of sustainability, and the computation of income from resource extraction has been subject to extensive discussion.

We assume that the economy is small and open in a strong sense. All prices, including interest rates, are assumed to be given from the world market. There are no restrictions on trade, and the nation's exports or imports, do not influence any price. Moreover, the capital market is perfect, so that there is no restriction on saving and borrowing at the given interest rates, provided that the long-run budget restriction is met.

3.3.1 Resource Rent

The resource rent is the share of the revenues from resource-based activities that can be attributed to the resource. Standard production theory predicts that with free entry, the profit will always tend to zero. If a firm is operating with positive profit, anybody can mimic its behaviour and earn the same profit. As more firms enter the market the profit is driven to zero; the revenues will only just cover the normal wages and return on capital.

Resource-based activities, from agriculture to oil production, do not have free entry. Only those with a reserve to produce from can extract oil, and only those with arable land can grow crops. In this case the profit can be positive – in excess of normal wages and return to capital – even in the long run. This extra profit is the resource rent: the part of the revenue that would not be possible without the resource.[1]

If the economy is completely open and all prices, including wages and return to capital, are determined abroad, the remaining part of national income can be realized independent of the presence of the resource. Even for an economy where resource extraction is the only sector, the resource rent would not be the entire income. Without the resource stock, the economy would have to use its labour force and capital stock for other purposes. In equilibrium the wages and return to capital would be the same (since they are assumed to be determined at the world market), and the only difference is the resource rent.

3.3.2 Resource Wealth

To simplify the notation and make the model more transparent, we assume for the moment that the interest rate is constant. As illustrated above, it is possible to generalize the model to non-constant interest rates, at least when future interest rates are known with certainty. We will return to this case below.

Let π_s for $s = t, t+1, \ldots$, denote the resource rent. Since the credit market is assumed to be perfect, this can finance a stream of consumption c_s where

$$\sum_{s=t}^{\infty} c_s (1+r)^{-(s-t)} \leq \sum_{s=t}^{\infty} \pi_s (1+r)^{-(s-t)} = W_{Rt}.$$

W_{Rt} is the resource wealth at time t. Clearly, if the wealth is unchanged from t to $t+1$, the sets of consumption streams which the wealth at time t and $t+1$ can finance, are identical.

---

[1]Positive profit is not only observed in resource-based industries. To maintain the claim that long-run profit is zero, many other rent concepts have been invented, such as monopoly rent, rent on technological advantages and rent on talents. For practical purposes they may be difficult to distinguish. Do OPEC (the Organisation of Petroleum-exporting Countries) earn monopoly rent or resource rent?

The Hicksian income is the amount the nation can spend during a year and still be as well off at the end of the year as in the beginning. We interpret 'as well off' as a requirement that it must be possible to maintain the consumption level. This is equivalent to defining the Hicksian income as the maximal consumption level that can be sustained infinitely, that is, the maximum sustainable consumption. With a constant interest rate this implies that the wealth should be constant, but, as discussed above, constant wealth is not a natural interpretation of 'as well off' if the interest rate is not constant.

For the moment we will assume that the interest rate is constant, and then total wealth must be constant. This does not require that the resource wealth is constant. Since the intertemporal consumption possibilities are determined by the wealth, the optimal policy is to deplete the resources to maximize resource wealth, and this policy will in general give non-constant revenues, and hence the resource well will not be constant. In this case, changes in resource wealth have to be compensated by other wealth components, for example, through financial wealth,[2] W_{Ft}. If these two are the only components of wealth, the total wealth is $W_t = W_{Ft} + W_{Rt}$.

With only these two wealth components, the part of the resource rent that is not consumed (c_t) must be accumulated as financial wealth, thus the financial wealth at time $t + 1$ will be

$$W_{F,t+1} = (W_{Ft} + \pi_t - c_t)(1 + r).$$

Similarly, from the definition of resource wealth, we find that

$$W_{R,t+1} = (W_{Rt} - \pi_t)(1 + r).$$

Adding the two equation we find that total wealth satisfies

$$W_{t+1} = (W_t - c_t)(1 + r).$$

---

[2]Since the interest rate is given, the optimal real capital stock is determined, hence investment in real capital cannot be used to compensate for the changes in resource wealth.

Maximum consumption subject to the constraint that wealth should be constant $W_{t+1} = W_t$ gives

$$c_t = \frac{r}{1+r}W_t = \frac{r}{1+r}(W_{Rt} + W_{Ft})$$

that is, the return to wealth.[3]

Note that the calculation gives the total national income and not just the income from resource extraction. On the other hand, the income can clearly be broken down into return on financial wealth and income from resource extraction. To concentrate on the income generated from resources, we consider the case where the financial wealth initially is zero, $W_{Ft} = 0$,[4] then maximum sustainable consumption is

$$c_t = \frac{r}{1+r}W_{Rt}. \tag{3.1}$$

Note that generally, without further restriction on the revenues, the maximum sustainable consumption c_t may be higher than current revenues π_t. The obvious example is a revenue path with $\pi_t = 0$, but where future revenues, π_t, for $t > 0$, are positive such that $W_{Rt} > 0$.

This approach to the calculation of Hicksian income is in a sense similar to the deduction of capital depreciation in the definition of NNI. To keep total wealth constant, reductions in resource wealth must be compensated with savings in financial assets. The required saving in financial assets must be deducted from revenues, to find maximum sustainable consumption. The changes in resource wealth are similar to the changes in capital stock, which is deducted from GNI.

---

[3]Note that the equation $W_{t+1} = (1+r)(W_t - c_t)$ means that the consumption occurs at the beginning of the period, and the remainder of the wealth gives a return r until the beginning of the next period. The return is then paid at the beginning of the next period, and the present value of this return is $r/(1+r)$. Thus the return to wealth is actually $(r/(1+r))W_t$ and not rW_t.

[4]For $W_{F0} \neq 0$ the return from the financial wealth would be added to the Hicksian income. Since this is already accounted for in traditional income measures, and since this component is not the topic of discussion here, we leave it out.

To summarize: the income from resource extraction depends on the wealth defined as the present value of the resource rent. Current resource rent matters only because of its contribution to the resource wealth, and the income from resource extraction will be positive if the wealth is positive, and may be higher or lower than current rent. This conclusion is different from some of the alternative proposals for measuring income, such as Repetto et al. (1989), who claim that the income from extraction of exhaustible resources will be zero unless new reserves are discovered, and El Serafy (1989) who argues that a share of current rent should be counted as income. Below we study the reasons for these differences.

3.3.3   Repetto's Depreciation Approach

One of the most cited methods of calculating income from natural resources is the one suggested by Repetto et al. (1989). In their calculation the depreciation is equal to the value of the changes in stock.[5] With no discovery of fresh reserves the depreciation is thus equal to the resource rent, and the income becomes zero. Only new discoveries will contribute to income. This conclusion is clearly different from the one derived above, where the income from resource extraction is positive as long as the present value of the resource rent is positive, independent of whether new reserves are discovered or not. In this section we will discuss the first part of Repetto's claim, that the income should be zero with no discoveries, leaving the treatment of discoveries to the section below on unanticipated changes in wealth.

The conclusion that resource rent should be excluded from income is not peculiar to Repetto et al. (1989). Similar claims are found in Dasgupta (1990), Hartwick (1990), Mäler (1991) and Pearce and Atkinson (1995). Most of this literature assumes a closed economy,

---

[5]The depreciation is the value of the changes in stock and is not equal to the changes in value of the stock. The effect of falling or increasing resource prices is thus not included.

which we will discuss in the next chapter, but the following simple open-economy model will illustrate some of the issues at stake, and the relation between Repetto's correction and the definition of Hicksian income presented in this chapter.

Consider the following continuous time model,[6] adopted from Gray (1914). A nation owns an exhaustible resource, with initial stock S_0. This resource can be sold at the world market at a constant price, p. The extraction cost depends on the rate of extraction x_t. The nation can also save money in foreign bonds at a constant interest rate. The total resource rent at time t is then the revenues px_t, less total costs $g(x_t)$.

This rent can be broken down into a Hotelling rent, and a Ricardian rent, as illustrated in Figure 3.2. The marginal cost of production is $g'(x_t)$. The Ricardian rent $g'(x_t)x_t - g(x_t)$ accounts for the fact that productions from some wells are cheaper than the marginal well. But due to the resource scarcity, there is a rent even on the marginal well, and this is the Hotelling rent $(p - g'(x_t))x_t$. It turns out that the maximum sustainable consumption this resource wealth allows is only the Ricardian rent,[7] and hence the Hotelling rent should not be included in the Hicksian income.

The wealth-based approach discussed above would include both the Ricardian and the Hotelling rent, not directly, but indirectly through the computation of the total resource wealth, thus

$$W_{Rt} = \int_t^\infty (px_s - g(x_s))e^{-r(s-t)}dt.$$

The two approaches appear to be different, since the conclusion above was that only the Ricardian rent should count, while the wealth includes

---

[6]The following discussion was initiated by a discussion with Geir Asheim.

[7]This claim follows from Hartwick's rule, to be discussed in the next chapter. It is essential to the conclusion that prices and interest rates are constant, since this makes the economy formally equivalent to a closed economy with stationary technology. See Hartwick and Hageman (1993) for a discussion of a similar model.

Figure 3.2 Ricardian and Hotelling rents in the Gray model

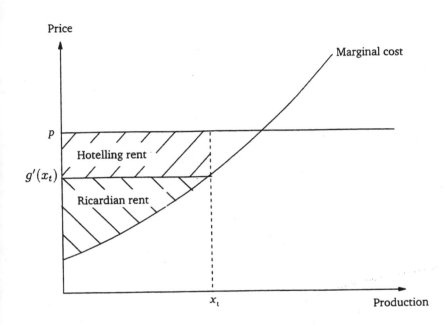

the present value of the Hotelling rent. Note, however, that the wealth approach computes the Hicksian income from the *present value* of rent, while the conclusion above was that the income is equal to the *stream* of Ricardian rent. Actually the two approaches are consistent, since the interest payment on the wealth is equal to the Ricardian rent,

$$rW_{Rt} = g'(x_t)x_t - g(x_t).$$

Repetto's calculations may be interpreted as an attempt to deduct the Hotelling rent. The weakness of this approach is that it may be difficult in practice to separate the Hotelling rent from the other components of the resource rent. (In addition to Ricardian rent, there may also be other rents, such as monopoly or oligopoly rent.) Moreover, the deduction of the Hotelling rent is only correct under rather strict assumptions, for example, it is essential that the nation has a stationary technology. This requires constant prices.

When the required assumptions are satisfied, and care is taken to deduct only the Hotelling part of the resource rent, the two approaches are equivalent. On the other hand, the wealth-based calculations are much more general, and do not require that the Hotelling part of the rent is identified. In practice, Repetto et al. (1989) appear to deduct too much of the resource rent, with the result that the resources are disregarded in the calculation of income. This would not be correct since, as El Serafy (1989) puts it: 'countries with marketable resources are evidently better off than those without such resources'.

3.3.4   El Serafy's User-Cost Approach

El Serafy (1989) proposes the user-cost approach as a method to compute the Hicksian income. El Serafy not only wants to adjust the income measure, he also claims that an adjustment of the gross production measure is needed: 'It is wrong to describe as current production that which is not current production. GDP is an important measure and much more in use than NDP (net domestic product)' (p.13).

As pointed out in the last chapter, national accounting measures have to meet a variety of different needs. Here we will focus on the measurement of income and welfare, and not on the measurement of total production. There are several conflicting objectives for measuring total production, too, but there are clearly cases where it would be wise to disregard the revenues from resource extraction. Resource extraction typically yields high revenues without much input of labour. In a model intended to analyse labour demand, the most relevant measure of total production would exclude these revenues.[8] A further discussion would

---

[8]In Norway, where the petroleum sector is large, resource extraction has typically been treated separately in macroeconomic business-cycle analyses. Usually onshore

require a separate analysis, which is beyond the scope of this book.

We restrict the attention to the interpretation as a measure of Hicksian income. In that context, I will argue that El Serafy's user-cost approach is a special case of the wealth approach, where he adds the assumption that the net price on the resource and the extraction rate are both constant.

El Serafy restricts the analysis to non-renewable resources. With a constant extraction rate, the length of extraction period, d, is equal to the reserves divided by extraction rate. To this assumption El Serafy adds the assumption that the rents are constant in real terms, that is, $\pi_s = \pi_t$ for all $t \leq s \leq t + d$. With this assumption the wealth is

$$W_t = \pi_t \frac{(1 + r) - (1 + r)^{-d}}{r},$$

and hence the Hicksian income is

$$\frac{r}{1 + r} W_t = \pi_t (1 - (1 + r)^{-(d+1)}) < \pi_t.$$

El Serafy thus suggests replacing π_t with $\pi_t(1 - (1 + r)^{-(d+1)})$ in the measurement of GDP. This adjustment will then in turn affect income measures such as NNI.

Is the assumption that resource rent should remain constant over a period of length d reasonable? This is only slightly more general than the assumption that production and net prices are constant. We consider these two assumptions starting with in turn, the assumption that net prices are constant.

How can the equilibrium price of a non-renewable resource be constant? As the remaining reserves approach zero the extraction rate has to decrease, the supply of resources will inevitably also decrease, and the prices must rise unless a suitable substitute is found. In a classic paper, Hotelling (1931) argued that a resource owner would want to extract all remaining reserves instantly unless the net price rose at least

---

GDP (GDP less value added in oil and gas depletion) is cited separately.

at a rate equal to the interest rate. Since the case where a resource owner extracts all his/her resources instantaneously cannot be an equilibrium, we conclude that in equilibrium net prices must be growing at a rate equal to the interest rate. This is known as the 'Hotelling rule'.

Hotelling (1931) pointed out several factors that would modify this conclusion, and the subsequent literature has demonstrated that there are many reasons for deviating from the simplest version of Hotelling's rule, (see Farzin, 1992). The empirical evidence is also somewhat mixed. Slade (1982) found empirical evidence for a U-shaped price path, with initially falling but eventually increasing prices, and Hall and Hall (1984) found evidence of increasing resource scarcity. Nordhaus (1992), on the other hand, presents price paths for many different resources, claiming that the opposite picture with decreasing real prices is the more typical one.

The assumption that prices are constant may be no more or less likely than other predictions. On the other hand, there is no reason to restrict attention to this specific case. The resource wealth approach allows us to consider any price assumption. In some cases non-constant prices may be more reasonable, and in any case it is interesting to be able to do sensitivity analysis on the price assumption.

If net prices do not increase at a rate equal to the interest rate, the resource owner will not be indifferent as to when the resource is extracted. With constant net prices, the optimal strategy is to extract the resource as fast as possible. The extraction path will then be determined by technical production capacity. In the early stages of extraction from some field, during the period when the production capacity is installed, no revenues are earned. At this stage current production is close to zero. Extrapolating this extraction rate is hardly a good prediction of actual production after the installations are complete.

In an example below we present estimates of Norwegian petroleum wealth. In that case, the wealth computed from actual production plans is more than twice that with a constant production profile. The actual production plans were based on technological information about the oil and gas fields. It is hard to see any reason to replace these plans with a constant production profile.

3.3.5 Unanticipated Changes in Wealth

In the discussion this far, we have assumed that future revenues are known with certainty. The discussion on the most reasonable assumption for these revenues illustrates that usually they are far from certain. Huge uncertainties are rather the typical picture. A telling example is that in 1981 the mean oil price forecast for 1994 was about US$110 per barrel (in 1994 US dollars, Manne and Schrattenholzer, 1988). The actual real price in 1994 was about US$17 per barrel. For an oil-producing country the resource rents that could be expected based on the mean 1981 estimate would be very different from the actual rents. Price fluctuation is typical for most natural resources. How do they affect the definition of income?

A natural extension of the resource wealth definition under uncertainty is to define it as the expected present value of future revenues.[9] Thus in the definition of the wealth at time t the rent at time $s > t$ is replaced with $E^t[\pi_s]$, where E denote expectations and the superscript t denotes that the expectations are taken at time t. The wealth at time t is then

$$W_{Rt} = \sum_{s=t}^{S} E^t[\pi_s](1+r)^{t-s}.$$

The actual changes in wealth, $\Delta W_{Rt} = W_{R,t+1} - W_{Rt}$, can be written:

---

[9]There is a good case for risk adjusting the discount factor, but since it is difficult to derive a theoretically satisfying model of this, I will leave it out in the following discussion. (The CAPM, and other models from Finance, suggests how to compute risk adjustments. These models consider assets that are traded on a market, but the market for resources in the ground is poorly developed.) A potential extension of Hicks's definition of income to the case of uncertainty is discussed below.

$$\Delta W_{Rt} = W_{R,t+1} - (1+r)(W_{Rt} - \pi_t) + r(W_{Rt} - \pi_t) - \pi_t \qquad (3.2)$$

The change in wealth is here broken down into three terms. The first one expresses changes in expectations. Note that under certainty,

$$W_{R,t+1} = (1+r)(W_{R,t} - \pi_t).$$

With uncertainty, future wealth is not only determined by current rent π_t and the return, but also from unexpected capital gains G_t, that is, shifts in the expectation. Using the definition of wealth, we find that

$$
\begin{aligned}
G_t &= W_{t+1} - (1+r)(W_t - \pi_t) \\
&= \sum_{s=t+1}^{S}(E^{t+1}[\pi_s] - E^t[\pi_s])(1+r)^{t+1-s}.
\end{aligned}
\qquad (3.3)
$$

From this expression we see that if the expected revenue at time $s \geq t+1$ is the same viewed from both time t and time $t+1$, that is, if $E^{t+1}[\pi_s] = E^t[\pi_s]$, then G_t will be zero, while if, for example, the price forecasts, reserve estimates or cost structure have changed from time t to $t+1$, then G_t can be substantial.

The second term in (3.2), $r(W_t - \pi_t)$, is the expected return from the wealth remaining after current extraction. There is no discounting of the current period's revenue in the definition of wealth, thus implicitly we have assumed that π_t is earned in the beginning of the period. Thus the resource wealth that gives the return during the period will not include current revenue. Finally the last term in (3.2) is the revenue from extraction at time t.

There are two possible views on how to treat G_t in income estimation. Either we can require that total wealth should be constant or that *expected* future wealth should be at least as large as the current wealth. Consider the first view. Since $W_{R,t+1} = (W_{Rt} - \pi_t)(1+r) + G_t$, the change in total wealth $W_t = W_{Ft} + W_{Rt}$ is

$$W_{t+1} = (W_t - c_t)(1+r) + G_t.$$

Requiring that $W_{t+1} = W_t$, and solving for c_t we find that

$$c_t = \frac{1}{1+r}(rW_t + G_t).$$

In other words, to keep wealth constant we can consume both the expected return rW_{Rt} and the unexpected capital gain G_t, both discounted one period. Since G_t is unrealized gains, the amount has to be borrowed unless the revenue π_t is sufficiently large.

Below we will demonstrate that with a similar procedure the adjusted national income of Norway would become negative in 1986, due to the fall in oil prices causing a fall in Norwegian petroleum wealth. But even in 1986, Norway was a rich country. There appears to be something wrong with an income concept that makes Norway's per capita income far lower than the income of most of the third world countries.

Repetto et al. (1989) argue that 'Treating unrealized capital gains and losses due to price changes as income is consistent with the definition of income given above, since the capital gain during the year could be consumed without reducing future potential consumption below what it would have been at the original price level'. With this procedure the income account will fluctuate sharply. Although Repetto et al. (1989) include only the capital gains from changes in reserve estimates, their income accounts for Indonesia from 1971 until 1984 varied between -0.3 billion rupiah in 1980 and 3.8 billion rupiah in 1974.

There are also important conceptual problems with this definition. We note from the definition of capital gain (3.3) that to compute G_t we need to know $E^{t+1}[\pi_s]$ for $s \geq t+1$. This information is not available at time t when the decisions on consumption and saving for period t have to be taken. In other words, with this definition we cannot know current income until it is too late to take it into account, that is, the current income, according to this definition, can affect only future consumption-savings decisions.

While W_{t+1} is not observable at time t the expected value $E^t[W_{t+1}]$

is. By the rule of double expectations, $E^t [E^{t+1} [\pi_s]] = E^t [\pi_s]$. It follows that $E^t [G_t] = 0$, and hence that

$$E^t [W_{t+1}] = (1 + r)(W_t - \pi_t).$$

Above we defined the Hicksian income as the maximum sustainable consumption, that is, the maximum subject to the restriction that $c_s = c_{s+1}$ for all $s \geq t$. The requirement that wealth should be constant was not imposed, but derived from the primary concept of maximizing sustainable consumption. To deal with uncertainty we must generalize the idea of maximizing sustainable consumption rather than working with a derived requirement of constant wealth.

A possible extension of maximal sustainable consumption to the case of uncertainty, would be the maximal consumption subject to $c_s = E^s [c_{s+1}]$ for all $s \geq t$. Since expected gains are zero, it follows as in Section 3.3.2, that if total consumption is

$$c_t = \frac{r}{1 + r} W_t \tag{3.4}$$

where W_t is total wealth including financial wealth, then $E^t [W_{t+1}] = W_t$, and hence $E^t[c_{t+1}] = (r/(1 + r))E^t[W_{t+1}] = (r/(1 + r))W_t = c_t$. Thus (3.4) gives the Hicksian income under uncertainty, and this expression is just as in the certainty case.

With the information available at time t, c_t is a known quantity while c_{t+1} is an uncertain one, with $E^t [c_{t+1}] = c_t$. A risk-averse person would then prefer the certain consumption c_t to the uncertain c_{t+1}. Thus even though expected future consumption is equal to current consumption, a risk-averse person will hold the future consumption prospects to be inferior to current consumption. An alternative to the requirement $c_t = E^t [c_{t+1}]$ is to introduce some ordering of risky prospects, and to require indifference between c_t and the prospects of c_{t+1}, as seen from period t according to that ordering. This concept is applied to the definition of sustainable development in Asheim and Brekke (1993). For simplicity we will use the risk-neutral case in the following.

3.3.6 Actual and Potential Income

A final complication is the choice of future policy. The resource rent is crucially dependent on the policy. The present value of actual resource rent may be considerably lower than the resource wealth that would have been possible with an alternative policy. For example, the resource rent from fisheries in Norway is currently close to zero, while it is computed that with alternative policies the rent may be increased to about 1 per cent of current GDP (Hanesson, 1991; Flåm, 1993; Kjelby, 1993). Maximizing the rent is, however, not the only the objective of the fishery policy. Much of the harvest is taken with small boats located in the rural northern areas. To increase resource rent, the employment in the sector has to be reduced considerably, and the main harvest would be taken with larger boats. This would conflict with maintaining the northern fisheries, which is an aim of the Norwegian fisheries policy. A more careful study of the rationale for this policy is beyond the scope of this book, but we have to consider which definition of wealth is most reasonable – is it the present value of future rent under the actual policy, or under the policy that maximizes the wealth?

To illustrate, consider the example of resource wealth from fisheries in Norway. We may consider the objective of maintaining the northern fisheries and employment in the fisheries sector as a constraint on optimization. Increasing the rent could then be impossible without violating the constraint. Alternatively, we may consider wealth as the present value under the policy that maximizes wealth (the maximal policy for short). When their revenues are lower than the corresponding income, the difference may be interpreted as governmental consumption, used to achieve specified goals of employment in fisheries.

The two definitions of wealth will give two different estimates of income from resource extraction. The return to the present value of actual resource rent denotes actual income while the income in the last case is denote potential income. Both income concepts will be interesting.

The easiest choice is to compute actual income. Let π_t^a denote the rent under the actual policy. For practical purposes is may be difficult to determine what the 'actual policy' will be in the future. There is no general method for dealing with that problem. Given π_t^a for all future years, the wealth is

$$W_t^a = \sum_{s=t}^{\infty} \pi_s^a (1+r)^{-(s-t)},$$

and the corresponding Hicksian income is $(r/(1+r))W_t^a$.

To compute the potential income, let π_s^{t*} denote the rent at time s along the path that is maximal at time t. Finally, let W_{Rt}^* denote the present value of revenues from a renewable resource when the resource is optimally managed. Formally

$$W_{Rt}^* = \sum_{s=t}^{\infty} \pi_s^{t*} (1+r)^{-(s-t)}.$$

The potential income is then $(r/(1+r))W_{Rt}^*$. But this income will be higher than total savings and consumption, since part of the income is 'lost' due to a policy that does not maximize resource wealth. The actual policy may still be optimal if the losses are incurred to meet objectives that are considered more valuable. Still, it would be interesting to estimate the loss.

To estimate the loss, we first note that since the actual policy is not the maximal policy, we would have to re-maximize every period, and hence the maximal rent for some future year s, as seen from year two different years t and $t+1$ will be different: $\pi_s^{t*} \neq \pi_s^{t+1,*}$. As a consequence,

$$W_{R,t+1}^* \neq (1+r)(W_{R,t}^* - \pi_t^*).$$

The right-hand side is what the wealth at time t would have been if a maximal policy had been followed, while the left-hand side is the maximum given the actual state at time $t + 1$. The difference between the left-hand side and the actual wealth, discounted to period t, is part of the loss due to a suboptimal policy. Moreover, during the period t the rent π_t^a is earned, instead of the rent π_t^{t*}. The total losses are

$$L_t = (\pi_t^{t*} - \pi_t^a) + (W_{Rt}^* - \pi_t^{t*}) - \frac{1}{1+r} W_{R,t+1}^*.$$

As above, we compute changes in total wealth, $W_t = W_{Ft} + W_{Rt}^*$. In this case we find that

$$W_{t+1} = (W_t - c_t - L_t)(1 + r).$$

We note that L_t is formally like consumption. If L_t is income that is forgone to achieve some other goal, it is in a sense consumed. Thinking of $c_t + L_t$ as total consumption, we see that maximum sustainable total consumption is the return to total wealth

$$c_t + L_t = \frac{r}{1+r} W_t.$$

The consumption L_t may not be constant, and hence ordinary consumption may also vary over time.

Devarajahn and Weiner (1991) apply a similar approach to the problem of soil degradation. With current mamagement, the soil becomes increasingly less fertile. Eventually, there will be nothing left to lose, and $L_t \downarrow 0$. Since savings are chosen to maintain wealth, total consumption $c_t + L_t$ will be constant, and hence ordinary consumption c_t will increase.

The maximum sustainable ordinary consumption when π_t^{t*} is considered infeasible, was found above to be $(r/(1+r))(W_t^a + W_{Ft})$. On the other hand, if we either change the extraction policy to realize the maximum wealth or consider L_t as consumption, maximum sustainable total consumption is $(r/(1+r))(W_t^* + W_{Ft})$. If L_t is considered as consumption, only the part $c_t = (r/(1+r))(W_t^* + W_{Ft}) - L_t$ is ordinary consumption and this part may not be constant or nondeclining.

3.3.7   Population Growth and Declining Interest Rates

With a growing population, constant aggregate national consumption would imply decreasing per capita consumption, and the nation will be impoverishing itself. Only with a constant population, is sustaining per capita consumption equivalent to sustaining aggregate consumption. To extend the analysis to a non-constant consumption, let n_t denote the population in the nation in period t.

In the analysis above we have further assumed that the interest rate is constant. This assumption is convenient, and useful to introduce the basic ideas of the wealth-based calculations of Hicksian income. Constant interest rates should not, however, be considered the canonical or generic case; rather it is reasonable to assume that the interest rate will be falling. To keep the consumption level constant at a global level, extraction of resources has to be compensated by increasing the stock of man-made capital. Assuming that the marginal return to capital decreases as the capital stock increases and increases as the resource use increases, both these effects tend to lower the interest rate, see Section 4.3 below. As Hicks noted, for a person not to impoverish him/herself, wealth has to grow when interest rates are falling. Thus to find the Hicksian income, we cannot compute the maximum consumption subject to the restriction that wealth should be constant, as suggested by, for example, Pearce and Atkinson (1990). Rather we must go back to the primary definition of Hicksian income as the maximum sustainable consumption.

How much wealth is needed to maintain for ever the per capita consumption level c, when interest rate is given by the path $(r_0, r_1, r_2, \ldots)$ and the population by the path $(n_0, n_1, n_2, \ldots)$? We assume that the paths both of interest rates and of population are known with certainty at the outset. First, define the discount factor from s back to t as

$$d_s(t) = \prod_{j=t}^{s-1} (1 + r_j)^{-1},$$

with $d_t(t) = 1$. The present value of a constant consumption stream is thus

$$\sum_{s=t}^{\infty} cn_s d_s(t) = c\sum_{s=t}^{\infty} n_s d_s(t) = cR_t$$

where $\sum_{s=t}^{\infty} d_s(t) = R_t$. Note that R_t may be infinite. For example, if population is constant, but the interest rate at some time T becomes zero, then $d_s(t) = d_T(t)$ for all $s \geq T$ and R_t will be infinite. With an infinite R_t the Hicksian income will be zero, unless the wealth is infinite too, in which case the income cannot be determined from calculations of wealth. In the following we will assume that the interest rate does not go to zero too fast so that R_t is finite.

Given the wealth W_t, the maximum sustainable per capita consumption is thus

$$c_t = \frac{W_t}{R_t}.$$

R_t is the cost of maintaining a constant per capita consumption $c = 1$, measured in terms of current consumption. Clearly, population growth will increase the cost of maintaining per capita consumption. Note further that since $d_s(t)$ is inversely proportional to $(1+r_j)$ for $t \leq j < s$, a falling interest rate means that R_t will be increasing, even with a constant population. The implication for this result is that with a lower interest rate, future consumption will be more expensive relative to current consumption, hence the cost of maintaining the consumption increases.

With some algebra we also find that the maximum sustainable consumption can be written as

$$c_t n_t = \frac{r_t W_t}{1 + r_t + (R_{t+1} - R_t)/n_t}.$$

If the population and interest rate are constant for all time, $R_{t+1} = R_t$ and the income becomes the well-known $(r/(1+r))W_t$ (remember that $c_t n_t$ is now aggregate consumption). On the other hand, if the cost of maintaining consumption R_t is increasing, the sustainable consumption is less than $(r/(1+r))W_t$. Thus, if the cost of maintaining the consumption increases, we would have to let the wealth grow over time, and to achieve this we would consume less than with constant interest rates.

The wealth will also depend upon future interest rates. The wealth of a revenue stream π_t is

$$W_t = \sum_{s=t}^{\infty} \pi_s d_t(s).$$

A negative shift in future interest rates will not only increase R_t but also the wealth W_t.

The conclusion that a growing wealth may be required to achieve sustainability, is in contrast to much of the literature on sustainable development. Pearce and Atkinson (1995) define sustainability as constant capital, and Repetto et al. (1989) use constant wealth as a definition of Hicksian income. These authors all assume, implicitly or explicitly, that the future interest rate is constant. As demonstrated in Asheim (1995), a declining interest rate is the generic case since the world economy depends upon exhaustible resources. Moreover, the world population is not expected to be constant.

3.4   PETROLEUM INCOME IN NORWAY

To illustrate the proposed definition of income, we consider two examples. These examples show some of the practical difficulties we would face if we were to adopt the ideas. The first example is the income from oil and gas extraction in Norway in the period from 1973 until 1989. We start with a short summary of the discussion in Norway concerning the use of petroleum revenues, illustrating the issues at stake.

Oil production started in Norway in 1973. During the first years, huge investments were undertaken, and the investment cost far exceeded the revenues, but higher income was expected in the future, and in the meantime, Norway tolerated huge deficits. A committee was set up to consider the extraction rate. In their report, they suggested that all the revenues should be saved in an oil fund, and that only the return on this fund should be available for current consumption. The surplus of the governmental budget was 'corrected for petroleum revenues', simply by subtracting the governmental revenues from the petroleum sector from the income side.

In 1988 a new committee introduced the wealth approach to compute the permanent income, or the Hicksian income. It found that the petroleum revenues in the early eighties far exceeded the permanent income, and thus concluded that the consumption had been excessive, since no petroleum fund had been established.

In Aslaksen et al. (1990) this computation was criticized for using information that would not have been available in 1980. It was pointed out that in the committee report, the wealth in the early eighties was computed in the light of OPEC III, that is, the fall in oil prices in winter 1986. Aslaksen et al. (1990) claimed that the policy of 1980 cannot be criticized for not using information that was unavailable until six years later. They then calculated the petroleum wealth using the information that had been available in the respective year, for example, the calculation of wealth in 1980 was based only on information available in 1980, and similarly for other years. The conclusion from this exercise was very different from the original one – the Hicksian income turned out to be two to three times higher than the actual revenues. This result is also very different from the adjustments proposed by El Serafy where the Hicksian income is always less than the current revenues.

Another interesting result was that the unexpected changes in wealth completely dominated the other components of changes in wealth. While the petroleum wealth was expected to increase throughout the 1980s, the wealth in fact fell dramatically. In 1981, the Hicksian income from petroleum wealth was about 30 per cent of GDP. Had Norway spent the entire Hicksian income during the early 1980s, there should have been a deficit on both governmental budgets and balance of payment. The debt in 1987 would have been larger than the remaining petroleum wealth, and the required reduction in governmental consumptions, would have been disastrous for the Norwegian economy. Fortunately, Norway was running a surplus both on governmental budgets and on the balance of payment. With OPEC III in 1986, the unexpected reduction in petroleum wealth was even larger than GDP. Had these capital losses been included in Hicksian income, the income would have become negative.

Table 3.1 Norwegian petroleum wealth 1973–89 (billions Norwegian kroner, 1986).

Year	Wealth	Unanticipated gains	Hicksian income	Rent
1973	47	428	3	
1974	456	−130	30	
1975	347	60	23	
1976	435	13	28	4
1977	451	−6	30	4
1978	474	504	31	9
1979	997	777	65	15
1980	1,827	239	120	40
1981	2,119	−233	139	45
1982	1,982	−88	130	46
1983	1,982	−441	130	57
1984	1,603	−460	105	77
1985	1,202	−731	79	84
1986	469	−219	31	23
1987	275	−106	18	19
1988	169	162	11	3
1989	325	—	21	27

To compute the wealth using only information that was available in the respective year, Aslaksen et al. (1990) based their calculations on price projections and production profiles from the governmental white paper for the respective years. The Norwegian petroleum wealth was then calculated for the period 1973 until 1988. The results are given in Table 3.1. Note that the numbers are recalculated to be consistent with the definitions above, and hence they are slightly different from the numbers in Aslaksen et al. (1990).

The first column is the wealth estimate, the second column (unanticipated gains) are the unanticipated changes in wealth, $W_{Rt+1} - (1 + r)(W_{Rt} - \pi_t)$, as in the decomposition of wealth changes in equation (3.2). The third column is the Hicksian income $(r/(1 + r))W_{Rt}$, and finally the last column is the rent π_t.

For most years the Hicksian income was higher than the rent. There are two reasons for this. First, prices were rising in the official price projections during most of the period until 1986. Thus the expected future rents are higher than the current rents. But the rising prices are not the only reason. Even in 1978, when future prices were expected to be constant in real terms, the Hicksian income was more than three times higher than the rent. The reason for this is that new fields were under development, and the production and thus also the rents were expected to increase.

To understand why high future production can make income higher than the rent from extraction, consider the case where no resources are extracted this year but the total remaining reserves are to be extracted during the next year. In this case the value of the current rent is zero, while the wealth may be considerable.

An observation on Table 3.1 that is perhaps more striking is the unanticipated changes in wealth. These changes depend on the difference $E^{t+1}[\pi_s] - E^t[\pi_s]$, which reflects how the evaluation of expected income in period $s \geq t + 1$ has changed from period t to $t + 1$. There are two main reasons why these expectations may change. First, new observation of oil prices may change the expected price path. Second, new information about the reserves may change the expected extraction path. The first point is the most important, since incidents like

OPEC I–III have considerably altered the view of future oil prices. But during the same period there have also been substantial shifts in both known and expected reserves, with a gradual but consistent movement upwards in both of them.

Confronted with unexpected changes of this magnitude it is natural to question the idea of Hicksian income in this context. For Norway to spend the entire Hicksian income would have required substantial deficits on the current account for the entire period, with a view to paying back the debt with future oil revenues. As these expected revenues did not eventuate, the national economy would have faced substantial difficulties. In short, spending the entire Hicksian income would have been hazardous.

3.4.1   Comparison with El Serafy

The previous calculations differ from the proposals of El Serafy (1989) on two points: actual production plans were used instead of assuming constant extraction and official price projections were used instead of assuming constant prices. That actual plans or constant extraction can make a difference is demonstrated by the estimates for 1978. In that year the official price projections predicted constant prices. Nevertheless, the Hicksian income was more than three times higher than the resource rent, while Hicksian income in El Serafy's analysis is always less than the rent.

In most years real oil prices were expected to grow at a constant rate from 1 to 2 per cent per year. These growth rates are in fact rather modest compared to the medium price projection from analysts all over the world (see Manne and Schrattenholzer, 1988). With hindsight we now know that these projections were wrong, but nevertheless the official price projections appeared modest at the time they were made.[10]

---

[10]Note, however, that the calculations are based on projections that were made for intermediate-run analysis. No official analysis was made of long-run budget constraints.

With rising prices, wealth estimates are obviously very sensitive to the growth rate. From 1983 to 1985 there were huge negative unexpected changes in wealth, even though real prices were almost constant in Norwegian kroner. The wealth in 1985 was only half the size of what was expected in 1983. The main reason for this is that the expected growth rate fell from 1.5 per cent to zero.

If we always assume zero growth, the wealth estimates will be more stable and the unexpected changes in wealth far less than those re-ported above.[11] On the other hand, if prices are actually believed to be increasing, then the wealth calculated under the constant price assumption does not reflect the expected long-run budget constraint.

3.4.2 Capital Gains

The changes in expectations are considerable. Treating these changes as income would have dramatic consequences for the measurement of national income. Since the positive change in 1979 and the negative one in 1985 are both larger than national income, the national income would have doubled in 1979 and become negative in 1985. Such measures would clearly give a wrong impression of the affluence of Norway. Note, that the main reason for these changes in expectations are the shifts in price forecasts.

In Section 3.3.5, we found that the Hicksian income under uncertainty was $(r/(1+r))W_t$, just as under certainty, but that this presumes risk neutrality. The calculation for Norway in this section shows that actually spending the entire Hicksian income would have had considerable negative consequences when the oil prices fell in 1986. Thus there is a strong case for taking risk aversion into account in the definition of Hicksian income under uncertainty, but this will have to be left as a project for future research.

---

[11]The same would be true for any growth rate, provided it is the same at all points in time.

3.5   SOIL DEGRADATION IN TANZANIA

The examples used in the discussion in this chapter have mainly been focused on the income from non-renewable resources. The approach presented is, however, much more general. To illustrate the application to other resources, I will in this section present some estimates of the required adjustments in national income to cope with soil degradation, a problem that is quite different in structure from natural resource extraction.

Natural resources such as oil, are not productive as a stock, only the extracted resources are used for production. Soil, on the other hand, is productive as a stock, but may degrade as a consequence of its use. We will apply the wealth approach to the problem of soil degradation in Tanzania.

The agricultural sector contributed 61 per cent of GDP in Tanzania in 1991. Even by Sub-Saharan African standards this share is high, and the fact that more than 80 per cent of the 24 million inhabitants depend on agriculture for subsistence, employment and income, underscores the central role of agricultural production both for national economic performance and for general welfare.

By the late 1980s the belief that the long-run growth potential of the sector was severely threatened by soil erosion and extraction of nutrients exceeding replacement rates (soil mining) had been widely adopted (Stoorvogel and Smaling, 1990). Physical and chemical properties of the soil have degraded as a result of the combined effect of poor farming practices and agricultural policies.

The problem of soil degradation has two main components: the loss of nutrients through soil mining, and the erosion of topsoil.

3.5.1   The Model

Suppose the production on one hectare (ha) of arable land is

$$Q_t = f(K_t, L_t, M_t, N_t, D_t),$$

where L_t is labour input, K_t is capital, N_t denotes nutritional content of the soil, M_t is material input, and D_t is root depth. The dynamic of real capital is

$$K_{t+1} = I_t + (1 - \delta)K_t$$

where I_t is investment and δK_t denotes capital depreciation.

The dynamic of the nutritional content of the soil is assumed to be

$$N_{t+1} = N_t + F_t - Q_t n - \beta E_t \tag{3.5}$$

where F_t is the input of nutrients from fertilizers, n is the unit content of nutrients in the crop, and βE_t is nutrient loss due to soil erosion. Finally the development in root depth is

$$D_{t+1} = D_t - E_t.$$

Note that unlike the development in nutrients, the reduction in root depth is irreversible, and hence E_t is non-negative.

As in the SLEMSA-model (Elwell and Stockings, 1982) we assume that erosion is decreasing the crop yield,

$$E_t = \phi \cdot \exp(\ bQ_t). \tag{3.6}$$

The model takes the choice of crop for each area as given. More crops will improve the plants' rooting system and protect the soil from the kinetic energy in rain drops, and thus more abundant crops will reduce erosion.

Let p_t denote the price of the crop, r the assumed constant interest rate, and let prices on fertilizers, material input and capital be normalized to 1. We will apply the model to an economy where markets are poorly developed and where there may not be an alternative use for all the labour input in the agricultural sector. In that case we may not be able to separate resource rent from labour income. To avoid this problem we let π_t denote the sum of resource rent and labour income

$$\pi_t = p_t Q_t - F_t - M_t - (r + \delta)K_t,$$

where M_t is the value of material input. The GDP contribution from the sector of study is $p_t Q_t - F_t - M_t$. We will apply the model to the agricultural sector in Tanzania, where the capital stock is rather small. π_t will then be approximately equal to the GDP contribution.

We may now use optimal control theory to find the production plan that maximizes wealth. Alternatively, we may, as discussed in Section 3.3.8, compute the wealth along an extension of the current, possibly not optimal, management policy. This last alternative allows us to estimate the disinvestment that soil erosion, with the current soil management, represents.

Let π_t^a denote the rent along a path extending current management policy. Then the wealth is as above

$$W_{Rt}^a = \sum_{s=t}^{\infty} \pi_s^a (1+r)^{s-t},$$

and the Hicksian income is $(r/(1+r))W_{Rt}^a$. Changes in the wealth is

$$W_{R,t+1} = (1+r)(W_{Rt} - \pi_t^a).$$

In Brekke et al. (1996) this model is used to study the maize production in Southern Highlands in Tanzania, with parameters partly computed from the 'soil productivity calculator', developed from field experiments by Aune and Lal (1994), and partly from guesstimates. Extending the current management policy was then interpreted as keeping the mix of input factor constant, which implies reducing the use of all input factors at the same rate as the reduction in root depth. We then found that the income was only 80 per cent of the rent, even when we disregarded population growth.

This result indicate that traditional income measures grossly overestimate the income from maize production in Southern Highlands. It should be kept in mind though that the model is rather stylized and that we had to use guesstimates on some parameters as the data for this area are poor. Note also that in this model, increasing crops is the only way to reduce soil erosion. For a further discussion of this analysis and some alternative scenarios, see Brekke et al. (1996).

3.6 SUMMARY

In this chapter we have presented a general framework for computing the Hicksian income. To find the Hicksian income, defined as the maximal sustainable consumption level, we first compute the wealth, W_t defined as the present value of future revenues. Next we need to compute the cost R_t, of sustaining a constant consumption $c = 1$, such as; with a constant interest rate $R_t = (1 + r)/r$. The Hicksian income is then W_t/R_t or, in the case of constant future interest rates,

$$\text{Hicksian income} = \frac{r}{1+r} W_t.$$

This method of computing the Hicksian income generalizes the user-cost approach suggested by El Serafy (1989). The wealth calculations are much more general, and apply equally well to exhaustible resources as to complex dynamic systems, such as soil erosion; moreover we do not have to assume constant prices or constant extraction rate. We also saw that in a case with stationary technology, the Hicksian income was equal to the income derived by excluding the Hotelling rent. This improves on Repetto et al.'s (1989) method, which deducts all rent, also the rent that should be included, moreover we do not have to separate the different kinds of rent. Furthermore, the stationary technology assumption is not needed.

While the wealth computation can be used to compute the wealth in any open economy, when all prices are determined on the world market, we have also seen that we face important problem when using this assumption in practice. The computation of petroleum wealth in Norway illustrated the problems that are caused by uncertain future prices. For the computation of soil wealth in Tanzania we had to make very crude assumptions about the dynamics of the soil quality. This need not to be taken as a weakness of the method. Uncertainty is a fact we have to face in long-term planning, and no method can free us from the uncertainty about the future. Similarly, degradation of soil quality is a complex process, and we are forced to make simplifying assumptions to analyse this system, no matter what methods we are using.

The main strength of the model is also its main limitation: the open economy assumption. More specifically, we assume that all prices are given at the world market. As pointed out in the introduction, this rules out the fundamental question of sustainability of the world economy. Especially if we assume that prices and interest rates are constant over time, important global questions are disregarded. The resource-rich economy can then deplete its resources at a rate which maximizes wealth, in the belief that whatever the economy would need of this resource in the future can be bought on the world market. If all resource-rich economies behaved in a similar manner, the world economy would eventually face resource scarcity. We have deliberately disregarded this fundamental issue of global resource scarcity, both to simplify the analysis, and because this important issue deserves a separate chapter, to which we now turn.

4. Income in the Closed Economy

We do not know how large the reserves are of non-renewable resources, but they clearly have to be finite. As remaining reserves decrease, the amount of extracted resources must decline, and we would have to move to reserves which have a higher extraction cost. While technological progress may reduce the resource use per produced unit and improved extraction technology can reduce the extraction cost, it is probable that eventually resource scarcity will cause resource prices to rise. As prices are exogenous in the open economy model, resource scarcity is a problem that has to be analysed in a global context, which is the ultimate example of a closed economy.

If all open economies consume no more than their Hicksian income, they would expect to be able to maintain their consumption infinitely. This is only possible if the consumption of the closed world economy can be extended infinitely. It is not obvious that it is at all possible to find a sustainable consumption level in a closed economy depending upon a non-renewable resource. That some resources are exhaustible is not sufficient to conclude that the development is not sustainable, since resource extraction can be offset with technological progress and capital accumulation. Theoretical studies of long-run growth perspectives have indicated that the substitution elasticity between exhaustible natural resources and capital is important for the sustainability of consumption. For a good discussion, see Dasgupta and Heal (1979, Chapter 7)

The purpose of this chapter is to study indicators for sustainability of the total world economy, and their relation to the income measure for the open economy. It is essential to the applicability of the model in the previous chapter that when every nation believes it's policy is sustainable, the world as a whole is on a sustainable path. Thus, the question we pose is: if the income measure indicated in the last chapter is adopted, is it possible that all countries believe that they are on a sustainable path, when in fact the world economy is not sustainable? If this is possible it would indicate a problem with the income measures above. To verify that this is not a problem, we must make sure that the income measures of the individual nations are consistent with the prospects for the entire world economy.

Note that we require that the world economy should be sustainable when *all* countries adopt a sustainable policy. This is a very strict requirement. It would be interesting also to know whether the world economy is sustainable even in the case where one or more countries' policies are clearly not sustainable. The total world economy is closed, and the question of sustainability of the closed economy has been studied in resource economic literature (see, for example, Dasgupta and Heal, 1979). The literature following the seminal papers of Weitzman (1976) and Hartwick (1977) indicates that sustainability requires a positive net investment. As we will see, this is unfortunately only a necessary condition, not a sufficient condition. Moreover, the literature is based on rather restrictive assumptions.

Net investment, in the literature following Weitzman (1976) and Hartwick (1977), is the total value of the changes in all capital stocks. Thus extraction of exhaustible resources should be offset by an investment in man-made capital of equal value, and therefore resource extraction would not contribute to sustainable consumption. On the face of it, there appears to be a tension between this conclusion and the results of Chapter 3, where the income from resource extraction was considerable. Fortunately, the two appraoches are fully consistent, as we will argue below. Part of the tension is due to the difference between open and closed economies moreover, the assumptions in the closed economy literature are much more restrictive than those of Chapter 3.

The wealth approach in the last chapter was formulated in discrete time and for an open economy. In this chapter we will extend this analysis to a closed economy and continuous time. The literature is quite technical, and so is the main body of this chapter even though I have tried to avoid technical issues as far as possible. For those who just want to learn the main conclusions from this chapter, the next section is a mixture of an introduction and an overview of the main results. The less technically inclined reader may want to read only Section 4.1, skip the rest of the Chapter, from 4.2 onwards, proceed directly to Chapter 5.

4.1   WEALTH IN A CLOSED ECONOMY

Based on Fisher's (1930) seminal analysis, the difference between the wealth in an open and a closed economy can be illustrated in a model with one good and two periods. In each of the periods $t = 1, 2$, only one commodity is consumed, thus consumption is a scalar c_t. The consumption path is a pair (c_1, c_2). In Figure 4.1, T is the set of feasible consumption pairs, and I is the indifference curve for a representative consumer, whose preferences over consumption pairs are represented by the utility function U. The optimal consumption path (c_1^*, c_2^*) is the one chosen from T to maximize $U(c_1, c_2)$.

The optimum is also the Walrasian equilibrium. In Figure 4.1, the line L represents both the iso-profit line of the firm and the budget line of the consumer, given the equilibrium prices (p_1, p_2). Thus, for all (c_1, c_2) on L,

$$p_1 c_1 + p_2 c_2 = p_1 c_1^* + p_2 c_2^* = m.$$

Given the equilibrium prices, the firm will maximize profit $p_1 y_1 + p_2 y_2$ subject to the technological constraint $(y_1, y_2) \in T$. Similarly the consumer will maximize utility subject to the budget constraint

Figure 4.1 Wealth in a two period model

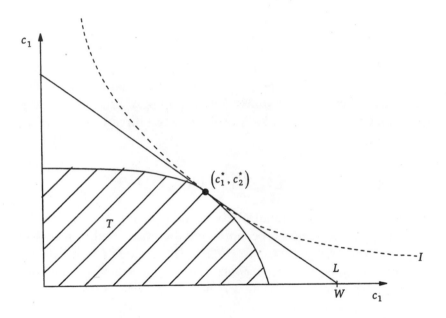

$p_1 c_1 + p_2 c_2 = m$. In equilibrium, markets must clear, and hence the solution to the two problems must be identical: $y_1^* = c_1^*$ and $y_2^* = c_2^*$.

Clearly, only relative prices p_2/p_1 matter, and we may thus normalize prices as we like. In the following we will choose the normalization $p_1 = 1$. We now define the wealth as the current value of future consumption, $W = c_1^* + p_2 c_2^*$. Introducing the interest rate $1 + r = 1/p_2$, the wealth becomes the more familiar

$$W = c_1^* + \frac{c_2^*}{1+r}.$$

Since production and consumption plans have to be equal, there is no opportunity to save or borrow. This is a crucial difference from the open economy. In both cases production is chosen to maximize profit

$$\max_{(y_1, y_2) \in T} y_1 + \frac{y_2}{1+r} \tag{4.1}$$

and consumption to maximize utility

$$\max_{c_1 + \frac{c_2}{1+r} = W} u(c_1, c_2). \tag{4.2}$$

The difference is that in the open economy, r is exogenous, and the production should provide only sufficient revenues to finance the consumption, that is,

$$c_1^* + \frac{c_2^*}{1+r} = y_1^* + \frac{y_2^*}{1+r}.$$

In the closed economy, on the other hand, r is endogenously determined by the market-clearing condition $(y_1^*, y_2^*) = (c_1^*, c_2^*)$. As a consequence we cannot separate the problems as in Chapter 3. With a perfect capital market, all consumption pairs within the budget set would be feasible for the open economy. Having determined the optimal production path, we could discuss how much a nation could consume and still be as well off at the end of the week.

For the closed economy, only consumption sets within the technology set are feasible. Given the optimal production profile (y_1^*, y_2^*) only one consumption path is feasible: $(c_1, c_2) = (y_1^*, y_2^*)$. Moreover, deviation from this path would change the equilibrium interest rate, r.

Hicksian income is the amount we *can* consume without impoverishing ourselves, but this amount may be different from *optimal* consumption. We would have to alter the preferences to move the optimal expenditure towards the Hicksian income, but this would also alter the equilibrium interest rate. Consequently, calculations of wealth cannot be used to determine the Hicksian income in this case.

The effect of an attempt to move expenditures towards the Hicksian income is illustrated in Figure 4.2. The original equilibrium is (c_1^*, c_2^*),

Figure 4.2 Shifting preferences in the closed economy

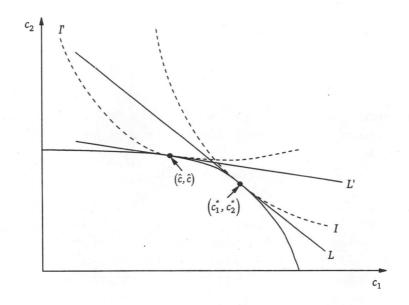

and the corresponding budget line and indifference curve are denoted by L and I. If the representative consumer wants to move to a sustainable consumption, he/she no longer prefers (c_1^*, c_2^*) to $(\hat{c}, \hat{c})$, and thus the indifference curve must have shifted to I', to support $(\hat{c}, \hat{c})$ as an equilibrium. The budget line must also shift to L'.

The difference between the income concept in the closed and the open economies is illustrated in Figure 4.3. In the closed economy, only the set T is feasible, while in the open economy the whole budget set is feasible. The Hicksian income, defined as the maximal sustainable consumptions is in this case $\hat{c}$. If the whole budget line L had been

Figure 4.3 Feasible consumption: Open and closed economies

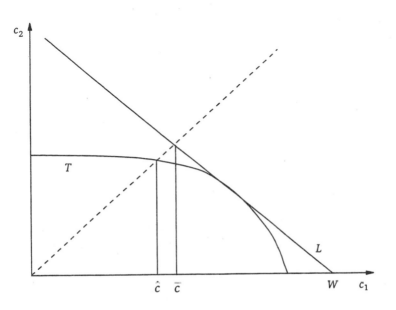

feasible, the maximum sustainable consumption would have been $\bar{c}$, which satisfies $\bar{c} + \bar{c}/(1+r) = W$.

A central issue in the multi-period case to be discussed in the next sections can be illustrated with the same figure. We then have to interpret the figure as representing an infinite horizon model. Think of c_2 as the average future consumption, while c_1 is current consumption. The closed economy under consideration is the whole world economy, with many utility maximizers. The equilibrium determines not only one interest rate and a consumption pair, but rather an infinite sequence of consumption and interest rates. In the figure we are only able to represent only the first interest rate and the average of future consumption. Since there are many nations, the prices and interest rates are considered given for each nation.[1]

Each nation can then compute its wealth, given these interest rates. Adding the consumption of all nations, we find world consumption, c_1. We denote the Hicksian income for a nation, as defined in Chapter 3, the Hicksian national income, to distinguish it from the Hicksian income for the world economy. Adding Hicksian national income for all the nations, gives us the quantity $\bar{c}$ in Figure 4.3. While $\bar{c}$ is not the true Hicksian income, we see from the figure that $c_1 > \hat{c}$ if and only if $c_1 > \bar{c}$. This appears to give us the desired conclusion: if the world as a whole uses more than the sum of Hicksian national income, then the world as a whole is using more than its Hicksian income, and vice versa. While Hicksian national income does not add up to the Hicksian income, the sign appears to be right.

This conclusion would be correct with only two periods, but here c_2 is an average of future utility. $\hat{c}$ is then the highest possible consumption subject to the constraint that average future consumption should be at least as high as current consumption. The Hicksian income is the highest sustainable consumption, which requires that $c_1 \leq c_t$ for all $t \geq 1$. Thus the Hicksian income is no larger than the highest consumption subject to the constraint that the *minimum* of future consumption should be at least as high as current consumption. Since the minimum may be strictly less than the average, sustainability is a much stronger requirement than $c_1 \leq c_2$, and hence the Hicksian income for the world economy may be less than $\hat{c}$. Comparing c_1 and $\bar{c}$ can thus only be used to determine that some paths are non-sustainable, but cannot be used to verify that a path is sustainable.

This case is illustrated in a three-period case in Figure 4.4. The equilibrium in a three-period model is a set of prices, here represented by the two interest rates, between periods 1 and 2 and between period

---

[1] To extend the model to many utility maximizers, the set of paths preferred to (c_1^*, c_2^*) should be interpreted as the set of potentially Pareto-improving paths.

Figure 4.4 Maintaining consumption, individually and collectively

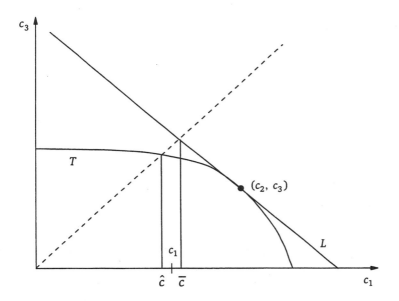

2 and 3. The equilibrium is also a consumption and production plan for each nation, such that production maximizes present value, and the consumption maximizes utility subject to the budget constraint. We concentrate on the trade-off between the second and third periods. The equilibrium consumption for the first period, c_1, is indicated on the c_2 axis. T is the set of feasible consumption paths (c_2, c_3) given that c_1 has been chosen in the first period, and the tangent line is the sum of the budget lines for all nations.

From the figure we see that the equilibrium aggregate consumption path (c_1, c_2, c_3) satisfies $c_2 > c_1 > c_3$. For simplicity, we assume that all nations are equal, so that a similar inequality applies to each nation's consumption. This inequality implies that no nation *plans* to sustain the consumption level c_1 during all three periods, but all of them believe that *if they wanted to*, they would be able to sustain the consumption level. This belief is based on the fact that $c_1 < \bar{c}$. If all pairs (c_2, c_3) on the budget line L had been available, then $\bar{c}$ would be the maximal sustainable consumption for the two last periods. Since the individual nations consider all pairs at the budget line to be feasible, and since $c_1 < \bar{c}$, each nation consumes less than its Hicksian national income, and hence they all believe that they are able to maintain consumption.

Still the aggregate world consumption is not sustainable. The maximum sustainable consumption level for the total economy is $\hat{c}$. Since $\hat{c} < c_1$, it is infeasible for the total world economy to maintain the consumption c_1. Does this imply that the definition of Hicksian income in Chapter 3 is inconsistent with our definition of Hicksian income in the closed economy? The answer is both yes and no.

In Chapter 3, the prices were independent of the behaviour, and we asked whether the nation could sustain the consumption if it wanted to, we did not have to specify the planned consumption for each nation. In the closed economy, the future consumption plan for all nations is a part of the specification of the intertemporal equilibrium. If in an equilibrium all nations' consumption plans are non-decreasing, they are all consuming less than their Hicksian national income. In the case above, they plan to behave non-sustainably. If one small economy instead chooses to deviate from this plan and instead chooses a sustainable consumption plan, the effect on the interest rate may be negligible and the shift would be feasible for this single nation. Since Chapter 3 focused on a single nation, the analysis is consistent with the story above.

The situation is different if all nations then decide to behave sustainably, however. Then the equilibrium would change, and so would the Hicksian national income in all nations. The calculations in Chapter 3 are contingent on a particular equilibrium, while Hicksian income for the closed economy is the maximal sustainable consumption, and in general the equilibrium aggregate consumption plan is not the particular consumption path that gives maximum sustainable consumption.

A final point is that for adding Hicksian national income, all nations must compute their Hicksian income with the same assumption about future prices. While the figure is in two periods, the calculation must in fact be made with an infinite number of periods, and future interest rates are thus essential to the wealth calculations. Since these future interest rates are not observables, different nations may in practice make different assumptions, and the sum of their Hicksian national income would not have any natural interpretation.

4.1.1   Sustainability and Net Investments

The sum of Hicksian national income and of consumption is not readily available. Can we study global sustainability without computing these numbers? Three cases where alternative measures are available are known from the literature. The first two are based on a result due to Weitzman (1976), while the last one is due to Hartwick (1977) and is called Hartwick's rule.

In a seminal paper, Weitzman (1976) showed that if the interest rate is constant and the technology is stationary, then $c_1 < c_2$ if and only if net investments are positive. In this model, c_2 is an average of future consumption in the sense that a constant consumption stream at the level c_2 will have the same present value as the future equilibrium consumption. The model requires that all kinds of capital are taken into account, including natural capital. It turns out that for consumption to be sustainable the Hotelling rent should not be consumed. This result requires that the interest rates for the entire future is known to be constant. But if we know the future prices, that is, the interest rates, why do we not know the future consumption? If we do know the future consumption we do not need an indicator to tell us whether $c_1 > c_2$, or not.

A version of this result, see Mäler (1991), is based on the assumption that the current equilibrium corresponds to the maximal discounted utility with a constant discount rate. The same result holds in this model: if resource rent is not reinvested, then consumption is not sustainable, in the sense that $c_1 > c_2$. To derive this conclusion, it must be assumed that the observed equilibrium is the consumption path that maximizes discounted utility with a constant discount rate. Unfortunately, there is no way of verifying this assumption.

Hartwick (1977) demonstrated Hartwick's rule, which tells us that if we actually do reinvest resource rent for all time, then consumption will be constant. In this case we also have to have knowledge about equilibrium in the distant future, since we need to know that net investment is zero along the entire equilibrium path. If we know net investment in the distant future, why do we not know the consumption?

All these approaches require extensive information about the distant future, and their empirical relevance is questionable, but nevertheless, these models are important. All these models represent cases where the resource rent should be excluded from sustainable consumption altogether, while in Chapter 3 we found that the Hicksian income from resource extraction may even exceed the resource rent. Why does resource rent not contribute to the Hicksian income in a closed economy, when we found that the present value of resource rent contributed to the Hicksian income for an open economy?

The answer is that even if the world as a whole has to reinvest resource rent to maintain consumption, it does not follow that each single nation has to reinvest the nation's share of the total resource rent to maintain the nation's consumption. With increasing resource scarcity the interest rate will decline, and all nations will have to increase their wealth to compensate. If all nations behave sustainably, even countries with no resources will have to contribute to the reinvestment, since their wealth must also increase.

Remember that all economies should use the same prices. Since the interest rate now is endogenous, we cannot assume a constant interest rate. Taking this into account, we introduce the *intertemporal cost of sustaining consumption*. With the good of year one as numeraire, it will take more wealth to maintain a given level of consumption, the lower the interest rate is. Formally the cost is

$$R(r, c) = c + \frac{1}{1+r}c.$$

This cost of sustaining consumption is increasing in $1/(1+r)$, and hence decreasing in r. The higher the interest rate is, the more we can get from current wealth.

From an intertemporal perspective, the real wealth should be deflated at the intertemporal cost of sustaining consumption. This deflation is very different from the deflator used to calculate real quantities in the SNA. Moreover, to compute this deflator we would have to know future prices and interest rates.

In the next section we will elaborate on and verify the claims made in this section. For this purpose we start with an extension of the wealth concept to an infinite horizon and continuous time.

4.2 EXTENDING THE WEALTH CONCEPT

In the first section we considered wealth in a two-period model. For the purposes of this chapter we need to define wealth in continuous time and infinite horizon.

4.2.1 Infinite Horizon

The definition of wealth in infinite horizon is essentially identical to the procedure in Section 4.1. The technology will now describe a convex subset in the set of infinite consumption paths, $(c_0, c_1, \ldots)$. Preferences are defined over such paths. Assuming convex preferences, maximizing the utility of the representative consumer gives the same outcome as the general eqilibrium with prices $(p_0, p_1, \ldots)$. With these prices the profit-maximizing production plan $(y_0^*, y_1^*, \ldots)$ is equal to the path that maximizes utility $(c_0^*, c_1^*, \ldots)$, given the budget constraint. As above, we normalize so that $p_1 = 1$, and define $1 + r_t = p_t/p_{t+1}$, for $t \geq 1$. Now the wealth becomes a present value, and the budget set is the paths $(c_0, c_1, \ldots)$ such that

$$\sum_{t=0}^{\infty} \left[c_t \prod_{s=1}^{t} (1 + r_s) \right] < \sum_{s=0}^{\infty} \left[y_t^* \prod_{s=1}^{t} (1 + r_s) \right] = W_0$$

where W_0 is the wealth. Similarly, we define the wealth in any period t as

$$W_t = \sum_{s=t}^{\infty} \left[c_s^* \prod_{k=t+1}^{s} (1 + r_k) \right] \tag{4.3}$$

All feasible paths have a present value less than or equal to the wealth, and the preferred paths are all more expensive, that is, have a present value larger than the wealth.

4.2.2 Continuous Time

Models in discrete time are conceptually simpler than in continuous time, but the mathematics of continuous time is much more powerful and as a consequence most of the theory is developed for continuous time models.

As above, we may define the technology as a set, T, of feasible consumption streams, but for the following discussion we need to be more specific. Let k_t denote the stock of capital and c_t the consumption at time t. The technology is now specified as a requirement that $(c_t, \dot{k}_t) \in S_t(k_t)$, where $S_t(k_t)$ is the set of feasible choices of consumption and investment at time t given the capital stock k_t, where k_t may be a vector. Given the initial capital k_t, the technology T is the set of all consumption paths c_t for $t \geq 0$, such that there exists a corresponding capital path k_t for $t \geq 0$ with $(c_t, \dot{k}_t) \in S_t(k_t)$ for all $t \geq 0$.

The general equilibrium prices are now a continuum, one price p_t for all $t \geq 0$. As above, we normalize so that $p_0 = 1$. The wealth will now be

$$\int_0^\infty c_t p_t dt \leq \int_0^\infty c_t^* p_t dt = W_0.$$

We define the interest rate as

$$r_t = -\frac{\dot{p}_t}{p_t},$$

then

$$p_t = \exp(-\int_0^t r_s ds). \tag{4.4}$$

The wealth at time t is

$$W_t = \int_t^\infty c_s^* p_s ds = \int_t^\infty c_s^* \exp(-\int_t^s r_u du) ds,$$

that is, the wealth is the present value of future consumption. All consumption paths that are feasible have present values less than or equal to the wealth and all that are strictly preferred are more expensive. Thus if $\tilde{c}_t$ for $t \geq 0$ is some consumption path that is preferred to c_t^* for $t > 0$, then

$$W_0 < \int_0^\infty \tilde{c}_s \exp(-\int_0^s r_u du) ds.$$

In the previous chapter we noted that with constant population, constant wealth was only sufficient for sustainability when the interest rate is constant. A constant interest rate is also essential to one of the models discussed below. In the current model, however, the interest rate is endogenously determined and depends on both technology and preferences. That the interest rate in equilibrium should be constant is a very restrictive assumption.

4.2.3 Intertemporal Cost of Sustaining Consumption

In Chapter 3, we defined the cost R_t of maintaining per capita consumption in the discrete time case. This was defined as the cost of maintaining a constant consumption equal to 1, for ever. We can now extend this to the continuous time case,

$$R_t = \int_t^\infty 1 \cdot n_s \exp\left(\int_t^s r_u du\right) ds$$

where r_t is the interest rate and n_t is the population. We will denote R_t as the intertemporal cost of sustaining consumption. R_t measures how much wealth it takes, measured in current consumption, to maintain per capita consumption $c_t = 1$. To maintain another consumption level, $c_t = c$, would take cR_t, and hence the maximal sustainable consumption given the wealth and future interest rates is W_t/R_t.

Note that if n_t and r_t are constant, then $R_t = n/r$, for all t, and hence the total Hicksian national income for a nation with total wealth W_t is $nW_t/R_t = rW_t$. In this case R_t is constant, and it is optimal to keep the wealth constant.

4.3   THE BASIC RESULTS

In the literature there are basically two related discoveries that are relevant for the definition of Hicksian income in the closed economy. These are due to Weitzman (1976) and Hartwick (1977). The work by Weitzman (1976) derives a welfare interpretation of the net national product, or net national income in the SNA 1993 terminology. Hartwick (1977) derive Hartwick's rule: consumption is constant for ever if and only if the net investment is zero at all future points in time. This requires that the resource rent is reinvested, and hence that the resource rent does not contribute to the closed economy income. A similar result can be derived from Weitzman's (1976) analysis. These conclusions are apparently in sharp contrast to the analysis of the previous chapter, where the income from resource extraction was found to be positive and potentially very large.

4.3.1 NNP as a Welfare Measure

The model of Weitzman (1976) does not explicitly include natural resources. On the other hand we may think of natural resources as a component of the capital stock in this model, especially since technology is assumed to be stationary. Including natural resources in the capital stock, the changes in the value of this stock must count as investment (or rather disinvestment, if the stock decreases).

Let c_t denote the consumption at time t, and k_t denote the capital stock. Consumption is a scalar, while the capital stock may be a vector; we can keep track of several stocks of capital, including stocks of natural resources or natural capital. The net investment is $\dot{k}_t$; the time derivative of the vector of capital. Given the capital stock, the technology determines which pairs of consumption and net investment are feasible. The technology is represented by the set $S(k_t)$, of feasible consumption-investment pairs,

$$(c_t, \dot{k}_t) \in S(k_t).$$

Subject to this restriction, c_t is chosen to maximize the present value of future consumption,

$$\int_t^\infty c_s e^{-r(s-t)} ds.$$

This may be interpreted as discounted utility with a linear utility function, but a linear utility function is not reasonable. Alternatively we may think of it as total wealth. As discussed above, the equilibrium consumption path is also the path that maximizes wealth subject to technical feasibility. Since it is assumed that the interest rate is constant, the implicit assumption is that intertemporal preferences are chosen so that constant interest rates are in fact the equilibrium with the given technology.

Let (c_t^*, k_t^*) denote the optimal path. Weitzman demonstrated that the solution to this problem satisfies

$$c_t^* + p_t \dot{k}_t^* = r \int_t^\infty c_s^* e^{-r(s-t)} ds, \qquad (4.5)$$

where p_t is the shadow price on capital measured in units of current consumption. Identifying the left-hand side as net national income (or net national product in Weitzman's terminology), and the right-hand side as welfare, he concluded that net national income is a welfare measure. We return to the measurement of welfare in this model in Chapter 6. Here we are interested in the possibility of sustaining current consumption.

We introduce the shorthand notation $Y_t = c_t^* + p_t \dot{k}_t^*$ for the NNI. Note that for any constant X it is true that $X = r \int_t^\infty X e^{-r(s-t)} ds$, thus (4.5) can be rewritten as

$$r \int_t^\infty Y_t e^{-r(s-t)} ds = r \int_t^\infty c_s^* e^{-r(s-t)} ds. \qquad (4.6)$$

One way of reading this is that if we replace the optimal consumption path with a consumption path that for all future is constant at the current level of NNI, that is, $c_s = Y_t$ for all $s \geq t$, then the present value would be preserved. Y_t is the variable that in Section 4.1 we referred to as average future consumption c_2.

The last equivalence seems to indicate that it is possible to maintain for ever a consumption equal to current NNI, but, as Weitzman pointed out, this conclusion is in general false, since this consumption path may be infeasible. Y_t should rather be interpreted as the 'stationary equivalent', that is, as the stationary consumption path with equal current value, or equal utility if utility is linear. On the other hand, if $p_t \dot{k}_t^* < 0$, then $c_t^* > Y_t$, and it follows from (4.6) that $c_t^* > c_s^*$ for some $s > t$. In other words, *if net investment $p_t \dot{k}_t^*$ is negative, the equilibrium path is not sustainable.* Thus negative net investment is a sufficient condition for non-sustainability in this model. Unfortunately, the converse is not true, since Y_t is an average of future consumption and hence $Y_t > c_t$ does not imply that $c_s \geq c_t$ for all $s \geq t$.

The stock of non-renewable resources has to be included in the capital vector, otherwise technology would not be stationary. For non-renewable resources the term $p_t \dot{k}_t^*$ would correspond to the value of the extracted resources. Thus, unless this extraction is compensated by investment in other capital stocks, the development must be non-sustainable

Svensson (1986) demonstrated that it is essential to this model that the rate of interest is constant. If maximization of the present value of consumption is interpreted as wealth maximization, the assumption is that the interest rate, which corresponds to an endogenous equilibrium price, is constant. To verify this assumption, we need to know the entire equilibrium price path, and then we would also know whether the development is sustainable or not. Alternatively, we may think of it as maximizing discounted linear utility, with a constant discount rate. In this case the assumption that utility is linear is very strong, but, as we will see below, that assumption can be relaxed.

Note also that the application of this model to an open economy, requires that there are no changes in terms of trade. Changes in terms of trade will change the technology S, which is assumed to be constant. This is especially important when the model is extended to resource extraction, since equilibrium prices on resources will increase as the resource becomes more scarce (the Hotelling rule).

4.3.2 Sustainability and Non-linear Utility

There is currently a growing literature based on Weitzman's framework, where resource extraction and environmental degradation of different kinds are specified, see Hartwick (1990), Mäler (1991) and Usher (1994).

Weitzman's analysis has been extended to maximization of discounted non-linear utility, $\int u(c_t)e^{-\delta t}dt$. With this extension, the strong assumption that interest rate is constant is replaced by the assumption that the utility discount rate is constant. In this literature, natural capital is also brought explicitly into the analysis. A simple variation on this type of model is the following. There is only one commodity produced, and the production function is

$$y_t = f(k_t, l_t, x_t),$$

where y_t is the quantity produced, k_t is the stock of capital, and x_t is resources extracted, all at time t. The stock of the resources is denoted s_t and

$$\dot{s}_t = -x_t.$$

The one commodity may be used either for consumption or for investment, thus

$$\dot{k}_t = y_t - c_t.$$

Subject to these constraints, discounted utility is maximized

$$\int u(c_t)e^{-\delta t}dt.$$

According to the maximum principle, the optimal solution can be found by maximizing the current value Hamiltonian at each point in time. The Hamiltonian is

$$H_t = u(c_t) + p_t\dot{k}_t - \mu_t x_t$$

where p_t and μ_t are the prices on capital and resources, respectively. Mäler (1991) demonstrated that the result in Weitzman (1976) can be extended[2] to show that

$$H_t = u(c_t^*) + p_t\dot{k}_t^* - \mu_t x_t^* = \delta \int_t^{\infty} u(c_s^*)e^{-\delta(s-t)}ds. \qquad (4.7)$$

---

[2]The result can be extended to the maximization of discounted utility with constant discount rate. Formally the problem is maximizing $\int u(x,a)e^{-\delta t}dt$ subject to $\dot{x}_t = f(x_t, a_t)$, where a is the control variable and x is the state variable. The Hamiltonian of this problem is $H = u + \mu f$, where μ is the shadow price on x. The optimal control maximizes H, and, assuming an internal solution, $H_a = 0$. (Subscript denotes differentiation.) The maximum principle also tells us that $\dot{\mu} = \delta\mu - H_x$, and hence $H_x = \delta\mu - \dot{\mu}$. Heuristically, by differentiating H with respect

Thus Mäler argues that H_t may be considered a welfare measure. We will return to this interpretation below in Chapter 6, after the discussion of welfare in the next chapter. For the current discussion we use (4.7) to generalize Weitzmans notion of a stationary equivalent. We define the stationary equivalent of the optimal policy as the consumption level $\bar{c}_t$ that gives the same discounted utility as the equilibrium path

$$\int_t^\infty u(\bar{c}_t)e^{-\delta(s-t)}ds = \int_t^\infty u(c_s^*)e^{-\delta(s-t)}ds.$$

From (4.7) it now follows that $H_t = u(\bar{c}_t)$.

As above, we see that if $p_t \dot{k}_t - \mu_t x_t < 0$, then by (4.7) $u(\bar{c}_t) = H_t < u(c_t^*)$, and it follows that for some $s > t$, the utility must be less than current utility $u(c_s^*) < u(c_t^*)$, and since the utility is increasing in c, this implies that $c_s^* < c_t^*$. Hence if the resource rent $\mu_t x_t$, is not reinvested in man-made capital, then the equilibrium consumption path is eventually decreasing.

The nice thing with this model is that conclusions about the long-run sustainability of the economy can be inferred from the value of current investment. We do not have to make predictions about prices in the distant future, as we had to do in the wealth calculations in Chapter 3. As we demonstrated in Chapter 3, changes in the price projections could cause huge fluctuations in the income estimates. The current model avoids this problem. Why does this approach need much less information about the future?

A part of the answer is that results from optimal control theory are applied to make inferences about how the future is reflected in current prices, but this is only a part of the story. The model further assumes

---

to t, we find that

$$\dot{H} = H_x \dot{x} + H_a \dot{a} + \dot{\mu}f = (\delta\mu - \dot{\mu})f + 0 + \dot{\mu}f = \delta(H - u)$$

which is a differential equation for H. Adding some transversality condition, the solution to this differential equation is $H_t = \delta \int_t^\infty u_s e^{-\delta(s-t)}ds$. Thus the Hamiltonian is proportional to optimal discounted utility.

that the demand side of the economy can be described as a representative consumer maximizing discounted utility with a constant discount rate. Thus the model requires strong assumptions about the distant future. For example, it is assumed that along a constant consumption path, the marginal rate of substitution between c_t and c_{t+x} is equal to the marginal rate of substitution between c_s and c_{s+x}, for arbitrary t, s and x. This assumption about future marginal rates of substitution has replaced the assumption about future prices.

The conclusion that the Hamiltonian is equal to the utility of the stationary equivalent $H_t = u(\bar{c}_t)$ further requires that the maximization of the Hamiltonian has an interior solution. This excludes, for example, that extraction of resources is limited by production capacities for the mine or field. In many applications resource extraction will actually be determined by geology and production capacity. The calculations of Hicksian income from petroleum extraction in Norway also show that the production profile is very important to the wealth estimates, and this production profile is determined by capacities and geology. This makes the restriction to cases with internal solutions problematic for applied purposes.

4.3.3   Hartwick's Rule

The study by Hartwick (1977), gives a similar result. The present discussion will be based on a generalization of this rule due to Dixit, Hammond and Hoel (1980). The equilibrium consumption path will depend on the shape of the technology and the preferences. Suppose that preferences are such that the equilibrium solution is actually a constant consumption path. For example, this would be the equilibrium with maximin preferences.

With the technology as described above, the equilibrium would be represented by a path of consumption c_t^* and capital k_t^* and investment $\dot{k}_t^*$, and a corresponding path of equilibrium prices p_t. Hartwick's original rule is that along such an equilibrium path, consumption is constant if the value of investment, $p_t \dot{k}_t^*$, is zero for all t. This result was generalized by Dixit, Hammond and Hoel, who proved that consumption is constant if and only if investment $p_t \dot{k}_t^*$ is constant for all t, but they also demonstrated that under reasonable conditions, this constant investment level had to be zero.

Consider a path that satisfies the ordinary Hartwick's rule, that investment is zero. Extraction of non-renewable resources is negative investment. According to Hartwick's rule, a constant consumption path is only possible if this negative investment is compensated by an equal positive investment in other capital stocks. The investment in other stocks has to be equal to the resource rent, a conclusion that is very similar to the conclusion from Weitzmans model.

Note that Hartwick's rule refers to the whole path. The claim is that a path has constant utility, if and only if the investment is constant *for all* $t \geq 0$. Suppose that the equilibrium path has zero investment at time 0. At time 0 this is all that is observable. Asheim (1994) has demonstrated that we cannot from this conclude that the current utility can be maintained for ever. The intuitive explantion of this conclusion is that if the utility is decreasing, then future generations, will be poor and hence their demand for resources will be low, too. The current value of resources will be low, reflecting this low future demand. As a consequence, the compensatory investment will be too low to maintain utility. To apply Hartwick's rule, we have to know the value of the investment for the entire infinite horizon. But if we have to predict the future investment path, we may as well predict the future consumption path to see if the utility is maintained. Why should predicting investment be easier than predicting consumption?

4.3.4 A Synthesis

All the models in this section link sustainability to compensating the disinvestment in natural capital with an investment of equal value in man-made capital. Moreover, all the models required that some variable was constant: the interest rate, the utility discount rate or the net investment in current value. The three cases can all be illustrated in a common figure.

Figure 4.5 Hartwick's and Weitzman's models

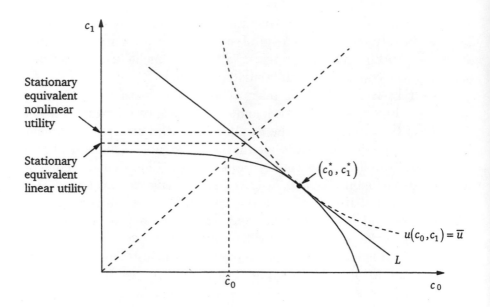

In Figure 4.5, c_0 denotes the current consumption, while c_1 is future consumption. In Weitzman's model we could think of c_1 as either $c_1 = \int_0^\infty c_t e^{-rt} dt$, or defined by $u(c_1) = \int_0^\infty u(c_t) e^{-t} dt$. In Hartwick's model we assume constant consumption $c_t = c_1$ for all $t > 0$. T denotes the technology as above. If the equilibrium is below the 45° line, then the development is non–sustainable. Hartwick considers the case where preferences are chosen so that the equilibrium is constant consumption, that is, the point $(\tilde{c}_0, \tilde{c}_1)$. In Weitzman's models, however, we may have an equilibrium at (c_0^*, c_1^*), with $c_0^* \neq c_1^*$. With a restriction on either the equilibrium interest rate, that is, the tangent L, or on the utility discount rate, we know that $c_0^* - c_1^*$ is positive if net investment is negative and vice versa. If $c_0^* > c_1^*$, we know that the development is not sustainable, while if $c_0^* < c_1^*$ we cannot conclude that the development is sustainable, since c_1^* is only an average of future consumption.

4.4 INCOME FROM NATURAL RESOURCES

All the different models in the previous sections support the same conclusion: positive net investment is a necessary but not sufficient condition for sustainability. To keep net investment positive, the value of extracted exhaustible resources should be invested in other capital stocks, and cannot be consumed. This is the basis, for example, Dasgupta's (1990) claim that an economy living solely on the extraction of non-renewable resources has an NNP equal to zero. This is appearently in conflict with the analysis in Chapter 3, where we found that resource extraction can make a significant contribution to sustainable consumption. Is there a real conflict?

The model of the previous section differed from those of Chapter 3 on several issues except for the difference between open and closed economies. To conclude that positive nct investment is necessary for sustainability, some form of constancy was assumed. While this assumption is essential to the conclusions and hard to verify, it does not help to explain why we found in Chapter 3 that resource extraction could add to sustainable consumption. The calculations in Chapter 3 can also be made with, for example, a constant interest rate - actually a constant interest rate was assumed in the applications.

A point that can explain the difference is the assumption that maximization of the Hamiltonian has an interior solution. To derive the conclusion that the value of extracted resources should be reinvested, we had to assume that there were no constraints on the rate of extraction of resources. This assumption may conflict with the calculations in Chapter 3.

In Section 3.4, the calculations were based on future extraction plans. Given the price expectation, if we disregard side constraint then the optimal production profile would be to extract the entire resource stock immediately. But there are side constraints besides the amount of remaining reserves. The actual plans were to a great extent determined by the physical structure of the oil fields. In one case, the Snorre field, the planned production was almost zero during one year in the middle of the production period, since the plan was to move the production platfor to another location. In other fields, water is pumped into the field to increase pressure, making it possible to extact a larger share of the field. These constraints on the extraction rate could be included in the Weitzman model by considering all relevant state variables (pressure at different locations in the well, amout of injected water, and so on) as part of the capital stock. We would then count the changes in these state variables, valued at the correct shadow price, as investment. Net investment would then be considerably different from the negative component of the value of extracted resources.

To net out the effect on these constraints, we assume that net prices satisfy the Hotelling rule. Then the oil producers would be indifferent as to when to extract the oil, and the technologial constraints would have zero shadow price. Nevertheless, calculation of Hicksian income, as presented in Chapter 3, would show a positive contribution to sustainable consumption, while the closed economy model would conclude that resource extraction should not contribute to sustainable consumption. The reason for this difference is the difference between a closed and an open economy. A variation on the model in section 3.3.3 may illustrate the point.

We consider an open economy with only two capital stocks, foreign bonds b_t and the resource stock s_t. Extraction costs are zero, and hence the Hotelling rule is that resource price p_t is increasing at a rate equal to the interest rate r. The problem is then

$$\max \int_0^t u(c_t)e^{-\delta t} dt$$

subject to

$$\dot{s}_t = -x_t$$
$$\dot{b}_t = rb_t + p_t x_t - c_t$$
$$\dot{p}_t = rp_t.$$

The Hamiltonian is

$$H_t = u(c_t^*) + \lambda_t \dot{s}_t^* + \mu_t \dot{b}_t^* + \nu_t \dot{p}_t.$$

As above it follows that the stationary equivalent is less than current consumption if $\bar{c}_t < c_t^*$, that is, if 'net investment' is negative. From the first-order conditions using the consumption goods as numeraire, we find that net investment is

$$b_t - p_t x_t + \frac{\nu_t}{\mu_t}\dot{p}_t.$$

Note that the price change $\dot{p}_t$ valued at a shadow price, is included in the 'net investment'. For the open economy, the price on the resource determines the productivity of resource extraction in terms of the numeraire consumption goods. The price is thus like a part of the captial stock, and the Hotelling rule makes this component positive. This is consistent with the conclusions of Chapter 3: while the resource rent $p_t x_t$ has to be reinvested, the return to the wealth $(\nu_t/\mu_t)\dot{p}_t$ may be consumed.

Note further that for those open economies which use the resource as input to production, the shadow price of the resource price will be negative. Summing over all open economies, the term $\dot{p}_t$ will vanish, as these price changes do not contribute to the sustainable consumption of the closed economy. In a model with agents owning only capital, resources or labour, respectively, Asheim (1986) demonstrates a case where it is the capital owner who has to reinvest the entire value of extracted resources. (See also Sefton and Weale, 1996 and Asheim 1996.)

We conclude that there is no conflict between the conclusions that positive net investment under certain conditions is necessary for sustainability, and the conclusions in Chapter 3 that resource extraction can make a significant contribution to sustainable consumption in an open economy. The two models are not competitors but complements. Models of the closed economy are useful for the study of the sustainability of the global economy, while the problem in Chapter 3 was to determine the maximum sustainable consumption for an open economy which is only a part of the global economy.

5. Welfare

Since the World Commission on Environment and Development (1987) introduced the term 'sustainable development' on to the political agenda, there has been a lively debate about the meaning of this term. The Commission (p. 47) defined sustainable development as 'development that meets the needs of the present without compromising the ability of future generations to meet their own need'. Two interpretations have been explored in environmental economics: 'weak' and 'strong' sustainability. Both these definitions have a substantially broader focus than just being able to sustain the consumption level as studied in Chapters 3 and 4.

The concept of weak sustainability presumes that we can construct a cardinal and comparable measure of welfare for successive generations, and that future technology and welfare functions may be predicted with reasonable accuracy. A development is then said to be weakly sustainable if the development is non-diminishing from generation to generation. This is by now the dominant interpretation of sustainability in environmental economics (see Solow, 1993, or Pearce et al., 1990).

The second interpretation, known as 'strong sustainability', sees sustainability as non-diminishing life opportunities (see Page, 1983 or Daly and Cobb, 1989, p. 72). This should be achieved by conserving the stock of human capital, technological capacity, natural resources and environmental quality. With weak sustainability human capital could be substituted for environmental quality, while strong sustainability would not allow such a substitution. The rationale for this stronger requirement is that we cannot know future preferences and technology with sufficient accuracy to evaluate how much human capital is required

91

to substitute for decreased environmental quality, we cannot even make sure that such a substitution is at all possible.

A central issue in this controversy is the possibility of measuring welfare in a manner that is comparable over time. This is not the complete picture, though, since even Daly and Cobb (1989), who defend strong sustainability, present an 'index of sustainable economic welfare'. Like many other such measures it is based on an adjustment of a national accounting aggregate, in this case of GDP. GDP is often interpreted as a measure of national welfare, and much of the recent criticism of GDP is based on a claim that GDP as currently measured does not reflect the welfare consequences of environmental degradation. But what is welfare and how can it be measured?

While the term 'welfare' is used repeatedly in economic writings, the precise meaning remains vague. The problem of defining individual utility or welfare has been a recurrent challenge to utilitarian ethics. Even more difficult, then, is the term 'social welfare': the welfare of society. Clearly, social welfare depends on the individual welfare of the members of the society, but is this all we need to know in order to determine social welfare? And how do we measure individual welfare?

The purpose of a national welfare measure, as GDP is claimed to be, is twofold. First, we want to know whether the current policy is improving welfare over time, that is, we want to compare national welfare at different points in time. This is especially important to the question of environmental degradation and sustainability, as explained above. Second, comparison of GDP between countries can be informative. These two kinds of comparison raise important problems that are different from those which arise when we try to measure the welfare consequences of alternative policies.

The measurement of social welfare raises many profound questions, some of which it would be far beyond the scope of the current book to study in their full depth. The questions involve both economics and moral philosophy. For an introduction to the relationship between economics and moral philosophy, see Hausman and McPherson (1996). In this chapter I will present an overview of the questions involved, and I will put special emphasis on the measurement of the welfare consequences of environmental degradation. Further I will focus especially on the problems of comparing welfare at different points in time, and between nations. In particular, I will argue that social welfare is not a unique quantity. Economic welfare theory sees social welfare from the perspective of an ethical observer or a benevolent dictator. The welfare will then depend on who the ethical observer is. Welfare is then not a unique quantity that can be measured.

To illustrate some of the special issues involved in the comparison of welfare over time, consider the following example. Suppose that you enjoy a meal of steak, c_1, and red wine, c_2. Your preferences over combinations of quantities of steak and wine are represented by the utility function $u(c_1, c_2)$. How much of the total utility $u(c_1, c_2)$ do you derive from the steak c_1 and how much from the wine c_2? Usually we would not find much sense in such a question, but when c_1 is reinterpreted as current consumption and c_2 as future consumption, we must ask a very similar question: that of comparing welfare over time. Typically, this problem is avoided by assuming time separability, for example, by assuming $u(c_1, c_2) = v_1(c_1) + \delta v_2(c_2)$, and by comparing $v_1(c_1)$ with $v_2(c_2)$. But the decomposition is not unique and, moreover, there are good reasons to believe that preferences are not time separable. This will be discussed below.

The comparison of welfare indicators between countries at the same point in time also needs some careful consideration. We would have to apply an assumption that is similar to time separability, for example, by assuming that cultural background is irrelevant to preferences. It is hardly a reasonable assumption. Refugees, who have to live in a society that is culturally very different from the one they come from, may find these differences more important to their welfare than material consumption and environmental conditions. How do we (and should we?) take cultural differences into account?

Individual welfare as well-being is a very general concept, and a measure of individual welfare should ideally take into account all things that make life worth living. This will hardly be a feasible approach. Perhaps it is too difficult to measure total welfare, and in much of the literature the qualifier 'economic' is added to indicate a more limited scope. For example, the term 'economic welfare' is also used in Nordhaus and Tobin's (1972) 'Measure of Economic Welfare', intended as an improvement on GNP as a measure of economic welfare. The term is used in later developments along the same lines, such as Daly and Cobb's (1988) 'Index of Sustainable Economic Welfare'.

To evaluate this tradition we must face the problem of how to separate economic welfare from total welfare. The first questions, then, are: what is the *economic* well-being of an individual? Does *economic* social welfare depend only upon the individual economic well-being? Under what conditions is a part of social welfare separable from total social welfare, and how do we identify the boundary between economic and non-economic well-being? Why do we need such a boundary at all?

I will argue that measures of economic welfare can often be seen as measures of the economic resources available, that is, income. The resources available in turn determine the nation capability of enhancing social welfare.

These and some other issues will be discussed in the following sections, but first we present the traditional position of economic welfare theory, the Bergson–Samuelson framework.

5.1   THE BERGSON – SAMUELSON FRAMEWORK

The Bergson–Samuelson framework was first put forward in a seminal paper by Bergson (1938) and was later explicated by Samuelson (1947). This is now the dominating paradigm of economic welfare theory and hence the natural starting point for a discussion of the measurement of national welfare. For a further discussion, beyond what is given here, see Atkinson and Stiglitz (1980), Starret (1988) or Mueller (1989).

Suppose you were a benevolent dictator. To choose the appropriate policy, you would need a *ranking* of social states. A social state is a description of the state of the society, and may include the private consumption of all individuals and the amount of public goods provided. For the moment we disregard public goods and let the social state x be a vector of individual commodity bundles, $x = (x_1, x_2, \ldots, x_I)$, where I is the number of individuals in the society.

The ranking of social states describes which states are socially preferable, that is, x is preferable to y if you choose x rather than y as a benevolent dictator. A social welfare function $W(x)$ is a numerical representation of such social preferences, that is, $W(x) > W(y)$ if and only if x is socially preferable to y. A welfare measure is any such numerical representation of social preferences. With this definition, a welfare measure may not have a unit of measurement.

Let $U_i(x_i)$ be a numerical representation of individual i's personal preferences, and $W(\cdot)$ a numerical representation of your social preferences. Suppose that as a benevolent dictator you want the social preferences to satisfy the Pareto principle: if nobody according to their personal preferences prefers y to x and at least one definitely prefers x to y, then x is socially preferred to y. Similarly, if everybody is indifferent to both x and y then x and y are equally important on the social preferences scale. Given these premises and a convexity assumption, it can be shown (see for example, Kreps, 1989) that there exists a function $V(\cdot)$ such that

$$W(x) = V(U_1(x_1), \ldots, U_I(x_I)).$$

The function V will depend on the chosen numerical representation of the individual and social preferences.

Comparing the consumption at the base year x^* with the consumption x, we find as a first-order approximation that,

$$W(x) - W(x^*) \approx \sum_{i=1}^{I} \frac{\partial V}{\partial U_i} \left(\sum_{n=1}^{N} \frac{\partial U_i}{\partial x_{in}} (x_{in} - x_{in}^*) \right)$$

where N is the number of commodities, and x_{in} is consumer i's consumption of commodity n. We assume that consumer i is maximizing utility subject to the budget set $px_i \leq y_i$, where y_i is the income of individual i. The first-order condition for utility maximization is

$$\frac{\partial U_i / \partial x_{in}}{\partial U_i / \partial x_{ik}} = \frac{p_n}{p_k}, \tag{5.1}$$

for all i, and all n, k. By normalizing utility for individual 1 we get $(\partial V / \partial U_1)(\partial U_1 / \partial x_{11}) = p_1$.

Further assume that as a benevolent dictator, you can redistribute income costlessly, so that you can choose all y_i freely, subject only to $\sum y_i \leq Y$, and that you want to choose the income distribution to maximize the social welfare W. The first-order condition for this maximization problem is to redistribute income so that each individual's consumption of an additional unit of good 1, would contribute equally to the social welfare. Combined with the above normalization, this implies that

$$\frac{\partial V}{\partial U_i} \frac{\partial U_i}{\partial x_{i1}} = p_1, \text{ for all } i. \tag{5.2}$$

Combining this equation with (5.1) we derive

$$\frac{\partial V}{\partial U_i} \frac{\partial U_i}{\partial x_{in}} = p_n, \tag{5.3}$$

for all i and all n. Inserting this into the equation for welfare changes we get,

$$W(x) - W(x^*) \approx \sum_{n=1}^{N} p_n \left(\sum_{i=1}^{I} x_{in} - x_{in}^* \right). \tag{5.4}$$

The right-hand side is the change in total consumption at market prices, that is, the national accounting measure of private and public consumption. With zero net investment, $\sum_n p_n [\sum_i x_{in}]$ would be the net national income. If the value of net investment reflects its contribution to future welfare, we have a rationale for NNI as a welfare measure.

A crucial assumption in this exposition is that you, as a benevolent dictator, could and did redistribute income costlessly. The actual income distribution in the society may be far from the one that you considered optimal. Moreover, the distribution that I (if I were a benevolent dictator) would consider optimal, may be very different from the one that you would consider optimal. Note that we are not merely trying to identify a Pareto improvement, but to measure welfare, and hence it is not sufficient to identify some side payment that makes everybody better off compared to the status quo.

If we knew that everybody in a similar position would make similar judgements, it would be possible to find a redistribution that is close to the optimum according to everybody's judgement. In many countries there is actually considerable redistribution of income. If this redistribution is a move towards what is commonly held to be the optimum, then this redistribution will make marginal utility more equal according to most people's judgements.

This argument presumes that the judgements we would make as benevolent dictators are similar. Even if this were so, it is not obvious that the redistribution within a country reflects an attempt to equalize marginal utility according to someone's judgement. Redistribution may equally well reflect the structure of power and political influence. Finally, redistribution is definitely not costless. All these issues suggest that we have to drop the claim (5.2) that marginal utility is equal for all i, and we would have to take income distribution into account to measure welfare (see 5.7.1 below, and also Atkinson and Stiglitz, 1980, and Drèze and Stern, 1987).

All the sources of ambiguity pointed out above are formulated within the Samuelson–Bergson approach, which has itself recently been subject to much criticism. Sugden (1993) states: 'For many years, the orthodox position in normative economics has been the one pioneered by Abram Bergson (1938) and Paul Samuelson (1947), and which now goes by the name "welfarism". But the tide of ideas is running strongly against this orthodoxy'. In the following I will give a brief review of some of the problems and criticisms that have been raised against the Samuelson–Bergson approach.

To construct a social welfare function, we need individual utility functions that are cardinal and interpersonally comparable. That such information is required is basically the conclusion of the extensive social choice literature, originating in Arrow's (1951) seminal impossibility theorem. For an excellent introduction to social choice theory, see Sen (1970, 1986).

5.2   WELL-BEING AND UTILITY

One important premiss of the Bergson–Samuelson welfare function is the idea that social welfare depends upon the well-being of the individuals of the society. Actually, the approach requires that this is all that matters to social welfare. We will return to this later, but it seems reasonable to assume that individual well-being must at least be one of the important aspects of a social welfare judgement.

I will use the term 'well-being' to refer to whatever is considered relevant as an input to a social welfare judgement, and let the term 'utility' denote a numerical representation of preferences. To reflect this distinction in the notation, we write the welfare function as

$$W(x) = V(\omega_1(x), \ldots, \omega_I(x))$$

where $\omega_i(x)$ is the well-being of i. Given such a distinction, Sen (1985b) asks whether individual well-being should be seen as utility.

A problem of this question is that 'utility' has several different interpretations. Sen (1985b) lists three possible interpretations: (1) happiness, (2) desire fulfilment, and (3) choice. The first two of these are the classical utilitarian interpretations, while the last one is the most popular among current economists. For a discussion of the first two see Sen (1985b), who argues that well-being should not be seen as utility in either of these interpretations. We will here discuss only the *choice* view of utility, for several reasons. First, because it is the dominating view on utility in modern economics. Second, and related, I know of no suggestions for measuring the welfare consequences of environmental degradation or resource extraction based on the first two views of well-being, while standard methods for valuing environmental quality are based on the choice view.

5.2.1 Revealed Preferences

In the choice view, utility is a numerical representation of a person's preferences, and the preferences represent the person's choice behaviour. That is, if x is chosen from a set containing both x and y, then x must be weakly preferred to y. The preference for x over y is revealed by the choice. A utility function is a numerical representation of the preferences; whenever x is preferred to y, the utility of x is at least as high as the utility of y: $u(x) \geq u(y)$.

To see well-being as utility means that the well-being function of i should represent the preferences of i. Thus

$$(\omega_i(x) \geq \omega_i(y)) \Leftrightarrow (u_i(x) \geq u_i(y)).$$

Well-being will then be seen as a measure of preference satisfaction. Given a numerical representation of the preferences, u_i, the well-being is, in this view, some monotone transformation of the utility $\omega_i = \phi_i(u_i)$. Even when we see well-being as utility we are not in business since we have to determine the different transformations, ϕ_i, one for each i. This can be broken down into two steps. First, we have to determine the cardinality of ω_i, which is equivalent to determining ϕ_i up to a linear transformation. Then we have to adjust all the transformations ϕ_i to make the different measures of well-being interpersonally comparable. We discuss each of these two steps below.

Why should we see well-being as utility? The most important argument that well-being should be taken as utility is that each individual best knows his/her own interest. If somebody chooses x rather than y how can we claim that his/her well-being is higher in y than in x. Hausman and McPherson (1996, Chapter 6) provide a critical assessment of seeing well-being as preference satisfaction. They point out that this view has problems with false beliefs, changes in preferences,

persons holding multiple conflicting preferences, and non-social preferences such as racism. Furthermore, maximization of individual well-
being is but one possible motive for choice behaviour. We will return
to this last point below, under the discussion of agency.

5.2.2　Cardinality

The choice view on utility is purely ordinal, but welfare analysis requires
a stronger utility concept. This has led to several attempts to derive
cardinal utility from choices. An overview of some attempts to measure
cardinal utility is mentioned in Tinbergen (1991). By far the most well
known is based on the expected utility approach. Given the axioms of
expected utility, von Neumann and Morgenstern (1944) proved that the
preferences over lotteries can be given a numerical representation which
is linear in probabilities. These representations are determined up to
a linear transformation, and may hence be taken as cardinal measures
(see for example, Harsanyi, 1955, 1987).

　　Sen (1976b) questioned to what extent these von Neumann–Morgenstern (vNM) utility functions represent a cardinal measure of well-
being. While the preferences can be given a representation that is
linear in probabilities, there are other representations which are not
linear in probabilities and which have a different cardinality. Sen questions why linear representation should be used as a cardinal measure
of well-being. The curvature of the vNM utilities determines the attitude towards risk; it is not obvious how this attitude is related to the
intensity of the preferences over certain outcomes. For a discussion, see
Weymark (1992).

5.2.3　Interpersonal Comparison

Even if well-being is seen as preference satisfaction, and a cardinal
measure of individual well-being is derived, a fundamental problem

remains: the interpersonal comparison of well-being.[1] If we see well-being as utility, $\omega_i(x) = \phi_i(u_i(x))$, and if, furthermore, u_i is a cardinal utility, the transformation must be linear: $\omega_i(x) = a_i u_i(x) + b_i$, with $a_i > 0$. But the parameters of the transformation may be different for different individuals. As an example, consider the case of utilitarianism: then

$$W = \sum \omega_i = \sum a_i u_i(x) + \sum b_i,$$

and the welfare effect of some change is crucially dependent upon the weights a_i. The determination of these coefficients requires interpersonal comparison.

In simple cases where the preferences are equal, a possible solution would be to assume that everybody has the same utility function. For example, suppose that individual i's utility of his/her income y_i is $u(y_i)$, where u is increasing and concave. If the total income in society could be freely redistributed so that y_i could be chosen subject only to $\sum y_i \leq Y$, then the optimum would be an equal income distribution, $y_i = Y/I$, for all i. If everybody had the same preferences, this may appear reasonable, but in real life there are many commodities, and different people have very different preferences.

To illustrate the problem, consider a society with two individuals, and with two commodities, a private good x and a common good E. Individual i's consumption of the private good is denoted x_i. The two consumers' preferences are represented by the cardinal utilities

$$u_1(x_1, E) = x_1 + 3E$$

and

$$u_2(x_2, E) = 3x_2 + E.$$

Consider the project that reduces both x_1 and x_2 with one unit, and increases E with one unit. With $\omega_i = u_i$ for both individuals,

---

[1] The view that interpersonal comparison is needed is not universally acknowledged (see Samuelson, 1977). See also Parks (1976), Kemp and Ng (1976), Sen (1970, 1979, 1986).

the social welfare is left unchanged by the project, since 1 gains and 2 loses the same amount of utility. However, $\omega_1 = u_1$, and $\omega_2 = u_2/3$, would represent the same preferences, but now person 1's gain will outweigh the loss of person 2. In a case like this where some lose and others gain, we would have to compare the losses of the losers with the gains of the winners. But how do we derive this required interpersonal comparison? In cost–benefit analyses it is standard to assume that the marginal utility of money is equal across individuals. While this assumption is convenient, there is no way to test it empirically. We will return to this assumption below, for now we are more interested in the source of the problem of interpersonal comparisons.

Within the revealed preference paradigm, the source of the problem is that choice cannot reveal which one of two persons is better off, since we cannot choose to become someone else. Nor can choice reveal whether one person's loss of utility is bigger than another person's gain. While we cannot choose to become someone else in reality, we can imagine making the choice, as a thought experiment. This leads to the idea of extended preferences (see Harsanyi, 1987, and also Arrow, 1977, and for a critique, see Broome, 1993). Extended preferences are a conceptualization of interpersonal comparison rather than an operational method for measuring interpersonally comparable utility. The problem of interpersonal comparison has been subject to considerable discussion (for example, see the papers in Elster and Roemer (eds), 1992). Unless we can find an objective basis for interpersonal comparison, social welfare will depend on who is the benevolent dictator. If social welfare depends on who makes the judgement, it is not a unique quantity, ready to be measured.

5.2.4　Agency and Well-being

Thus far we have assumed that we can see well-being as utility, but is that reasonable? Suppose that you are a benevolent dictator, and have to compare the social states x and y. You know that, given the choice,

i would choose x. Thus i's utility u_i must be higher in x than in y. Does this imply that in your welfare function $V(\omega_1, \ldots, \omega_I)$, you must give ω_i a higher value in x than in y?

At first glance it may appear obvious that the answer should be positive. Is not i's choice of x over y evidence that he/she judges his/her position to be better in x than in y? If i judges his/her position to be better in x than in y, why should anybody overrule this judgement? Is not i the best person to know what is good for i? Nevertheless, this is one of the questions where the Samuelson–Bergson approach has been subject to much criticism.

First, note that the question of whether well-being should be seen as utility, should not be mixed up with the issue of paternalism. In general, paternalism is, in some way or another, to induce somebody to behave differently from what they otherwise would, with the sole motive that this is in the person's own interest. In the current setting, the benevolent dictator considers a choice between x and y. If $\omega_i(y) > \omega_i(x)$, and $u_i(x) > u_i(y)$ while for all $j \neq i$: $\omega_j(y) = \omega_j(x)$ and $u_j(y) = u_j(x)$, we are in a position where the benevolent dictator would prefer the opposite of what i would choose, and the only reason for this preference is i's well-being. To *implement* y over x in this position, rather than giving i the opportunity to choose, is paternalism, but to *judge* x to be better than y, is not to overrule the individual's own choice, unless we actively induce him/her to change his/her choice for his/her own good (see also Hausman and McPherson, 1996).

Restraining from paternalism is an argument for decentralized decision making. In the market everybody chooses from his/her own budget set. It would be paternalistic to induce the economic agents to choose other commodity bundles for the purpose of increasing their own well-being. Environmental quality, however, is a public good, and the choice between two alternatives x and y, each having a different environmental quality, will affect all individuals. We cannot let a single individual i 'make his/her own choice' between x and y, without having this individual choose for everybody else, too. In this sense, we cannot fully decentralize the decision on the level of environmental quality. For a further discussion of paternalism, see Burrows (1993). Paternalism may not be an argument for seeing well-being as preference satisfaction in social welfare judgements, but are there any argument why we should see well-being as something different?

Note that for ω_i and ω_j to enter the same welfare function, they must be comparable. If the evaluation of i and $j's$ well-being is based on different standards of evaluation, it may not be reasonable to put them together in the same welfare function.

A critique of utilitarianism raised by Rawls (1971) is based on a claim that different people's utility is based on different standards of evaluation. Individuals i and j compare x and y according to their own plan of life. But these plans may be so different that we cannot sensibly put the two utility functions into the same welfare function. Rawls points out that a person, the benevolent dictator, who is to evaluate the position of another, would either have to evaluate the other's position according to his/her own life plan, but then the ranking may be different from the other person's own ranking, or, he/she has to adapt to the other's plan of life, but is he/she then still the same person? In Rawls's own words: 'The worth to us of the circumstances of others is not ... its value to them'.[2]

To be useful in a social welfare judgement, the utility of different individuals must in some sense measure the same thing. Rawls's point is that judgements about well-being for different combinations of characteristics and positions should be evaluated from some common point of view in order to be interpersonally comparable. But evaluation that is based on a common point of view, cannot be consistent with individual preferences that are derived from vastly different life plans. How then, can the utility of different individuals measure the same thing?

The following story may illustrate the problem:

Once upon a time two boys found a cake. One of them said, 'Splendid! I

---

[2]Rawls (1971, p. 174), see also Sugden (1993).

will eat the cake.' The other one said, 'No, that is not fair! We found the cake together, and we should share it alike; half for you and half for me.' The first boy said, 'No, I should have the whole cake!' The second said, 'No we should share and share alike; half for you and half for me.' The first said, 'No, I want the whole cake.' The second said, 'No, let us share it half and half.' Along came an adult who said: 'Gentlemen, you shouldn't fight about this; you should *compromise*. Give him three-quarters of the cake.' (Smullyan, 1980, p. 56. Italics in the original)

The proposed compromise becomes nonsense because it ignores the fact that the demands from the two boys are not comparable. The first boy may be seen as maximizing individual well-being while the second is acting as an agent for a fair distribution. To use utility functions to rationalize these demands, the first boy's utility must be increasing as his share of the cake increases, while the second boy's utility must reach a maximum when the distribution is equal. But these utility functions cannot serve as a basis for a social welfare judgement, since their motivation is so different that their numerical representation, the utility, would be incommensurable.

Another aspect of this problem with the concept of well-being as utility, is the presumed motives for behaviour. As pointed out above, the term 'revealed preferences' indicates that the preferences exist prior to the choice. Similarly, the well-being of a person must have some kind of separate existence if maximizing a function of it should have any normative appeal. To see choice behaviour as revealing well–being, implies an empirical assumption about human behaviour; maximizing personal well-being is the only motivation for human behaviour. While a person can derive well-being from doing the right thing, this should be distinguished from the agency aspect of a person.

Sen (1985b) argues that 'People have aspects other than well-being. Not all their activities are aimed at maximizing well-being (nor do their activities always contribute to it), no matter how broadly we define well–being within the limits of that general concept'. When the second boy above proposed sharing half and half, this should rather be interpreted as evidence that the second boy is acting as an *agent* for a fair distribution. When behaviour is seen as maximizing well-being, this ignores the ethical considerations behind human behaviour. Moral philosophy has always concerned humanity and is very important in most religions. It would be very strange indeed if such considerations had no impact on human behaviour. This leads Sen (1985b) to conclude that well-being should not be seen as utility.

Above we introduced a social welfare function as a representation of a person's preferences as a benevolent dictator. The construction of these social preferences presumed that everybody at the outset had clearly defined personal preferences. These personal preferences are conceptually different from the social preferences. Thus we have introduced two preference orderings for the same person: a personal and a social set of preferences. An interpretation of the example above is that the first boy expresses his personal preferences while the second expresses his social preferences. Even if we see well-being as preference satisfaction, it would not make sense to add well-being unless we make sure that comparable preferences are satisfied.

Moral philosophers have tried to develop alternatives to utility as a basis for social welfare evaluations. Rawls's concept of 'primary good' is explicitly introduced to simplify interpersonal comparisons. Similarly, Dworkin (1981) argues for an even distribution of resources, not utility. Nozik's (1974) classic book develops a conception of justice which has no use for individual utility or well-being. Sen (1985a) introduced the concepts 'functionings' and 'capability' as a basis for interpersonal comparisons. We will discuss the relevancy of these approaches to the measurement of the welfare effect of environmental degradation in Section 5.9.

5.3 SOCIAL WELFARE AND INDIVIDUAL WELL-BEING

If we were able to measure interpersonally comparable individual well-being, the next step would be to aggregate them into a measure of *social* welfare. Also on this point there are a wide variety of different opinions.

With a purely individualistic philosophy, any value judgement is some individual's value judgement (see Buchanan, 1954). An example is Nozik (1974), who even questions the intentions of those talking about social welfare. Observing that individually we are willing to accept losses at one point for gains at another, for example, we go to the dentist to avoid future pain or do unpleasant work for its results, he asks

> Why not, *similarly*, hold that some persons have to bear some costs that benefit other persons more, for the sake of the overall social good? But there is no *social entity* with a good that undergoes some sacrifice for its own good. There are only individual people, different individual people, with their own individual lives. Using one of these people for the benefit of others, uses him and benefits the others. Nothing more. What happens is that something is done to him for the sake of others. Talk of an overall social good covers this up. (Intentionally?).[3]

As an alternative to social welfare judgement, Nozik argues that justice should be defined in terms of just procedures for decision making, and not in terms of end-state evaluations. For those who share Nozik's position, social welfare is not a quantity to be measured. Most authors would not join Nozik, but rather hold that social welfare, although ambiguous, is relevant for discussions of social justice.

Note that we presented the Bergson–Samuelson approach in terms of a benevolent dictator. With this construction, the social welfare judgement is someone's judgement. No matter which procedures are used to

---

[3]Nozik (1974), p. 32. Italics in the original.

make decisions, the individuals who participate in decision making may base their decisions on some subjective social welfare judgement. The problem with this interpretation is that, social welfare measurement is not an objective quantity, ready to be measured. The ambiguity of well-being, discussed in the previous section, further underlines this. The move from individual well-being to social welfare also introduce some additional ambiguities.

First, there are different views on how to aggregate individual well-being. According to the utilitarian view, social welfare is the sum of individual well–being $W^j = \sum_i \omega_i^j$, but others use non-linear versions. There are also examples in the literature where the utility of individuals with different characteristics are weighted differently.[4]

The previous claim that a social welfare judgement depends on who makes the judgement is reinforced when we consider the aggregation of individual well-being into social welfare. Thus social welfare becomes

$$W^j = V^j(\omega_1^j, \ldots, \omega_I^j).$$

with a superscript j also on the function V. The aggregation function V thus represents a separate reason why social welfare will depend on who is the benevolent dictator. This subjectivity of social welfare is a problem for developing NNI or another national accounting measure of welfare.

5.4   GROWTH AND WELFARE

The comparison of welfare in different years has received little attention in the literature. If we see individual well-being as utility, this comparison is especially difficult, since changes in utility over time are not revealed by choices.

---

[4]For example Jorgenson (1993) weights household utility by its equivalence scale and not by the number of persons in the household.

In the simplest intertemporal model in Chapters 3 and 4, utility was defined as a function both of current consumption c_1 and of future consumption c_2. The total utility is $u(c_1, c_2)$. How can this utility function be used to answer whether the individual is better off now with c_1 than in the future with c_2?

The most common way of avoiding the problem is to assume that the preferences over consumption bundles in one period are independent of the preferences over consumption bundles in the other. Let $u_t(\cdot)$ be the utility function representing the ranking of possible consumption vectors at time t. This is consistent with the intertemporal model where total utility is the discounted sum $u(c_1, c_2) = u_1(c_1) + \delta u_2(c_2)$. Based on this assumption, the literature uses several ways of comparing utility at different points in time.

5.4.1 Intertemporally Separable Preferences

What does it mean that welfare is higher at time t than at time s? Usually, the question is answered with reference to some instantaneous utility functions, for example, by assuming that the person is better off at time t with c_t than at time s with c_s, if $u_t(c_t) > u_t(c_s)$. This is the standard method for intertemporal comparisons, and the basis for the computation of price indexes.

Suppose that c_t, for all t, is chosen to maximize the same utility function $u(c)$ subject to the budget constraint $c_t p_t \leq m_t$. A standard revealed preference argument tells us that if $p_t c_s \leq p_t c_t$, then $u(c_t) \geq u(c_s)$. Let us define the price index $P = p_t c_s / p_s c_s$. The claim that $p_t c_s \leq p_t c_t$ is then equivalent to $m_t \geq m_s / P$. If $t > s$, the price index P is the Laspeyre index, which allows us to conclude that welfare will increase if real income increases, while if $t < s$, P is the inverse of the Paasche index and allows us to conclude that welfare is will decline if real income declines. For a further discussion of price indexes, see Diewert (1987).

The construction of price indexes requires that the utility function

$u_t(\cdot)$ is the same in all years. If this is not the case, we have an ambiguity since we may have both $u_t(c_t) > u_t(c_s)$ and $u_s(c_t) < u_s(c_s)$ (see Graaff, 1957). This problem is usually avoided by simply assuming that the ranking are the same at all points in time. However, as pointed out by Sen (1976a) 'The sad fact is that even if the ranking is the same, we have an ambiguity'. This ambiguity arises for a reason similar to why interpersonal comparison is a problem.

The problem of interpersonal comparison within the revealed preferences paradigm arises because we do not choose our characteristics or identity. Any comparison of alternatives over which we do not choose, faces the same kind of problem. We can choose when to consume a particular good, but we cannot choose between being at two different points in time. We cannot choose between being at time t with consumption c_t or being at time s with consumption c_s. Even if I prefer c_t to c_s at both points in time, my utility might have been higher at time s, perhaps because I was in a better mood at that time.

Extending the model from two periods to an infinite horizon and continuous time, the assumption would be that the utility is of the form

$$U_t(C_t) = \int_t^\infty u(c_s) \exp(-\int_t^s \delta_r dr) ds.$$

Here C_t is the consumption stream C from t to infinity. We want to compare this with the utility of the same consumption stream, starting at t', but discounted to time t. The discounted utility would then be

$$U_t(C_{t'}) = \int_t^\infty u(c_{s-t+t'}) \exp(-\int_t^s \delta_r dr) ds.$$

The literature based on Weitzman (1976) uses $U_t(\cdot)$ as a basis for comparison of welfare at different points in time. In that strand of the literature, a person is said to be better off at t than at t' if $U_t(C_t) > U_t(C_{t'})$. Note, however, that to avoid the ambiguity pointed out by Graaff (1957) we have to assume that the discount rate is constant.

In both cases it is a fundamental assumption that total utility can be written as a sum. This assumption is dubious. The assumption

$u(c_1, c_2) = u_1(c_1) + \delta u_2(c_2)$, implies that preferences are intertemporally separable. The preferences over consumption vectors at time 2, are assumed to be independent of the consumption at time 1. However, there are good reasons to believe that previous consumption has consequences for how we perceive current consumption. On an individual level, previous consumption establishes habits. At a social level, the previous consumption pattern has influence on both social and economic institutions.

5.4.2 Intertemporally Non-separable Preferences

The standard assumption in growth theory, that preferences are intertemporally separable, was questioned by Hicks (1965, p 261). He claimed that

> If the successive consumptions have independent utilities, the amount of present consumption which the chooser will be willing to give up, in order to be able to increase consumption in year 5 from so much to so much, will be independent of the consumptions that are planned for years 4 and 6. It will be just the same, whether the increase in year 5 is to boost a sudden spurt out of line with its neighbours, or is needed to fill a gap, to make up a deficiency (that would otherwise have occurred in year 5), so raising the consumption of year 5 up to the common level. ... when stated in those terms, surely it must be said that it cannot be accepted.

One reason why preferences may be intertemporally non-separable is addiction. The preference at time t is influenced by the consumption patterns the individual has grown used to from the periods $s < t$. There is much evidence that addiction is a rather general phenomena at an individual level (see Kahneman and Varey, 1992).

A study of the consequences on non-separability in a standard growth model was presented in Ryder and Heal (1973). Recently there have been some empirical studies on this assumption (see for example, Braun et al., 1993). These studies clearly indicate that preferences are not intertemporally separable. Ryder and Heal (1973) assumed that the utility at time t depends upon both the consumption level and the historical consumption level,

$$u_t = u(c_t, z_t),$$

where z_t is a moving average of previous consumption;

$$\dot{z}_t = \gamma(c_t - z_t).$$

u is increasing in c_t and decreasing in z_t, since a person who is used to a high consumption level will, according to Ryder and Heal (1973), derive less utility from a given consumption than someone who is used to a low consumption level.

The individual, then, is assumed to choose consumption over his/her entire lifetime, to maximize discounted utility,

$$U(C; z_0) = \int_0^T u(c_t, z_t)e^{-\delta t}dt,$$

where z_0 is given, and z_t is as above. The total utility is an integral, just as with intertemporal separability. Nevertheless, the picture is very different from the time-separable case. First, c_t is not chosen to maximize $u(c_t, z_t)$, since a rational individual will recognize that c_t also influences future utility through z_s for $s \geq t$. Moreover, the preferences for consumption vectors at time t depend upon both past consumption and planned future consumption. Thus the preferences are different at different points in time, and the ambiguity pointed out by Graaff (1957) poses a problem.

To base intertemporal comparison of well-being on instantaneous utilities raises an additional problem here, since the instantaneous utility, $u(c_t, z_t)$ is not uniquely determined by the intertemporal preferences. For example, it is possible to choose a_t and b_t, such that

$$\int_0^T (a_t c_t - b_t z_t)e^{-\delta t}dt = constant,$$

where the constant is independent of the consumption path.[5] Let us define the utility function

$$\tilde{u}_t(c_t, z_t) = u(c_t, z_t) + a_t c_t - b_t z_t. \tag{5.5}$$

Now the discounted sum of both u and $\tilde{u}$ represents the same preferences. But is the utility at time t equal to $u_t = u(c_t, z_t)$ or $\tilde{u}_t = \tilde{u}_t(c_t, z_t)$? Moreover, if $u_t > u_s$ while $\tilde{u}_t < \tilde{u}_s$, is welfare then highest at t or at s?

If T is finite a possible solution to this problem is to insist on autonomous utilities. Note that in (5.5) there is a subscript t on $\tilde{u}_t$ but not on u. If we require that the utility function should be the same for all t, $\tilde{u}_t$ would be ruled out. With $T = \infty$, however, both a_t and b_t can be chosen to be non-zero and still be independent of t. It is thus not obvious that 'successive consumption has independent utilities', as Hicks put it.

5.4.3 Social Addiction

Adam Smith pointed out the importance of relative income, when he claimed that the clothing required for women to appear in public without shame was different in England and Scotland. Later Hirsch (1976), Frank (1985a), and Sen (1983), among others, have emphasized that relative consumption level matters for practical and psychological reasons. There are several models that would capture these effects, but for illustration, suppose that the utility is, as above, $u(c_t, z_t)$, but now we assume that z_t is the weighted average of the previous average consumption in society. To the individual, z_t would then be an exogenous

---

[5]The requirement is satisfied by first choosing b_t arbitrarily and then choosing

$$a_t = \int_t^T b_s e^{-\gamma(s-t)} ds.$$

parameter; a fact that he/she has no influence over. In this model the preferences over consumption bundles will change over time for a representative individual. Below we will discuss some indications that preferences do change over time in this manner. For a short survey of the evidence on the social dimension of consumption, see Frank (1985b).

Residents in many third world villages have no need for automobiles in order to participate in social and economic life, while a person living in Los Angeles cannot function normally without one. Similarly Sen (1993) argues that while average income in Harlem is higher than in Kerala in India even when corrected for cost of living, the population in Harlem is objectively poorer since it takes more resources to function normally in a richer society. These are practical reasons why relative income matters.

Dittmar (1992) studies the social psychology of material possessions. She argues that our material possessions are important to communicate to each other how we view ourselves. They are signals of how we see our social standing and with which groups we identify. Obviously it takes different amounts of resources to communicate the same message in different cultures or at different points in time. Thus, even if the preferences for consumption goods are the same at two different points in time, we cannot compare well-being at different points in time except on the basis of these preferences.

Easterlin (1974) demonstrated that own-rated happiness[6] was uncorrelated with income over time and between countries, but self-rated happiness increased slightly with an increase in income within a country and in the same year. If we accept self-rated happiness as an indicator of well-being, these results indicate that to the extent that income is important to well-being, then it is the relative income that is important. Only those who are rich compared to the average population are able to use consumption to signal membership of important groups. Unfortunately, it is not at all clear that self-rated happiness is a good indicator

---

[6]Own-rated happiness was measured in surveys where respondents were asked to rank their happiness in categories: very happy, fairly happy and not very happy.

of well-being, especially in time series or in a comparison between countries. The respondents may use the perceived happiness in the current society as an anchor for their responses, in the sense that the 'fairly happy' alternative is interpreted as average happiness. We would then expect average self-rated happiness to be constant over time, even if happiness actually does increase.

A related although very different study was conducted by Hareide (1991) on a Norwegian community where he showed that while per capita income has been increasing since the end of last century, other indicators such as suicide rates, crime rates, murders, consumption of alcohol and divorce rates, had been decreasing only until the 1960s. A decline in these indicators, according to Hareide, indicate less misery as we would expect. From 1960 until 1990 income continued to increase, but the misery indicators hav also been increasing sharply. That Hareide's misery indicators are rising may be seen as an indicator of declining welfare in spite of increasing income. This interpretation of the misery indicators may be questioned, though. The quality of the statistical data has improved considerably over time, and misery, in particular, was likely to be under-reported in earlier data. Still, results such as those of Hareide and Easterlin give reasons for having second thought about the standard assumption that welfare is an increasing function of income.

These questions are especially interesting in the study of economic growth and the environment from a welfare perspective. Environmental organization has questioned the 'materialistic life-style'; do we really need that much material consumption? Pezzey (1992) points out that: 'Given a definition of sustainability as non-declining welfare or utility, we are also concerned with the way that economic growth *creates* needs and wants'.

Frank (1985a) argues that the external effect from the consumption of positional goods will tend to move consumption from leisure time to material consumption, but that taxation of labour income reduces this effect. If this is true, taxation of labour income is actually a Pigouvian tax. Moreover, since the effect of this tax is to reduce material consumption, it is also a 'green' tax.

I do not claim that income does not matter to well-being; it obviously does. The point is simply that it is an oversimplification to assume that welfare at time t is a function $u(c_t)$ independent of the history. The well-being a person derives from material consumption cannot be analysed without reference to his/her consumption history and his/her social context.

5.5 INTERNATIONAL COMPARISON

The social dimension of well-being is also important for international comparison. To the extent that relative consumption matters to welfare, indicators such as GDP will overestimate the differences in welfare between countries. If it is true that a person in a third world village has less need of a car than a person in Los Angeles, then this is relevant for comparison of well-being in the third world village against well-being in Los Angeles.

In the simple model above, the effect of past consumption was represented by z_t. Comparing two countries, we would expect the z_t to be different since the consumption history of individual countries is different. Not only is consumption history different, but culture, religion, climate and topology may also be very different. All these variations will have an impact on utility. Moreover, differences in culture and religion make the Rawlsian criticism of welfare theory, as discussed in Section 5.2.4, relevant. With varying cultural backgrounds, typical life plans will also be very different, and as a consequence utilities will be less comparable between people in different countries, than between different people in the same country.

If we interpret GDP or a similar measure as a welfare indicator, and use this for comparison of welfare between countries, we would in effect ignore all these problems. Adjusting for resource extraction or environmental degradation would not help to solve them either. The differences in needs and preferences between countries are hardly so small that the errors we make by ignoring them are minor, but maybe these welfare indicators could be given a less ambitious interpretation as indicators of 'economic' welfare?

5.6 ECONOMIC WELFARE

Peskin (1996) claims that 'At best, as Prof. Hicks pointed out over 50 years ago, GNP could be an index of *economic* welfare. But economic welfare is not necessarily social welfare'. In Hicks (1940), which Peskin refers to, economic welfare is defined as welfare 'under the hypothesis of *constant wants*'. With this definition, economic welfare is just social welfare with given preferences, and not a more narrowly defined welfare concept as Peskin suggests. Can we define 'economic welfare' as some narrower concept of welfare, perhaps one that is easier to measure?

Nordhaus and Tobin's (1972) welfare-oriented adjustment of NNI was called the measure of economic welfare (MEW). The term has also been used in much of the literature following Nordhaus and Tobin's analysis. If economic welfare is interpreted more narrowly than social welfare, this raises two questions. First, which aspects of welfare are economic and which are not? Second, is it possible to break down social welfare into distinct components.

One possible distinction between economic and non-economic aspects of welfare is whether they are effects of economic production. This distinction is indicated in Daly and Cobb (1989), who deduct side-effects of production in their 'indicator of sustainable economic welfare'. But what are the side-effects of production? Are increasing crime rates a side-effect of increasing alienation, due to the organization of production? Individual and social addiction is clearly related to the consumption of modern consumer goods, which is definitely not independent of economic production. The fall of the iron curtain had economic as well as political reasons.

A very restrictive definition is that economic welfare includes only welfare derived from market goods, which would exclude effects of environmental degradation, urbanization, commuting to work and other aspects that are generally included in most proposed measures of economic welfare in the Nordhaus and Tobin (1972) tradition. On the other hand, if we use a wider definition it is hard to see why environmental degradation should be included while cultural changes and higher consumption standards should not.

We now turn to the second problem: whatever distinguishes economic from non-economic welfare, is it possible to consider one of them independent of the other? This would require that we distinguish between the well-being each individual derives from the economic and the non-economic part of his/her position. Finally, when we aggregate well-being, the aggregation of one component of it must be independent of the other.

At the individual level it is not obvious that economic well-being can be separated from non-economic well-being. A person's economic resources will influence his/her potential achievements in many other areas of life, and the preferences for consumer goods will be influenced by the person's general plan of life.

Even if it were possible to distinguish between the welfare derived from different components of a person's position, we also need to aggregate it into social economic welfare. Suppose it is possible to separate the two parts of individual utility, and suppose, moreover, that the total cardinal and interpersonally comparable utility for i is the additive sum of an economic and a non-economic component $u_i = u_{ei} + u_{ni}$. The Samuelson–Bergson social welfare function would then be $W = V(u_1, \ldots, u_I)$. Except for plain utilitarianism this welfare function cannot be broken down into an economic and a non-economic component such as: $W = V_e(u_{e1}, \ldots, u_{eI}) + V_n(u_{n1}, \ldots, u_{nI})$. With plain utilitarianism, this separation is possible, though, and the economic welfare would be

$$W_e = \sum_{i=1}^{I} u_{ei}.$$

We see that only with very strong assumptions is it possible to derive an economic part of social welfare that can be described by a Bergson–Samuelson welfare function. Alternatively we can interpret economic welfare as the economic *determinant* of welfare, not as the economic *part* of welfare. With this interpretation, economic welfare is *not* described by any welfare function, it is only a description of the economic part of the position of the individuals in the society.

In this view, economic welfare is income or wealth, perhaps in a rather wide sense. A similar view is expressed by Eisner (1988), who states that 'It must be quickly conceded that there are many aspects of human well-being that conventional economics accounts do not measure. ... Our account may better seek to measure, not welfare itself, but the nation's output of final goods and services which are presumed to contribute to welfare'.

Rawls's concept of primary goods (see Section 5.9, below) similarly focuses on the goods required to achieve welfare, or rather to realize the plan of life. In his philosophy, income and wealth are primary goods which a rational person would need to implement his/her plan of life. I will demonstrate below that some of the adjustments to GDP which Nordhaus and Tobin suggested to make it a better welfare measure, can actually be interpreted as a generalization of the Hicksian income definition, as discussed in Chapters 3 and 4.

5.7 VALUATION OF ENVIRONMENTAL QUALITY

Valuation of environmental quality is currently one of the major research areas in environmental economics. Recently it has also become the subject of much controversy. Mostly, this discussion has been related to the use of environmental values in project evaluation, and less for the purpose of measuring changes in overall social welfare, which is the reason why it is relevant in our context.

The literature on the valuation of environmental goods is growing rapidly. There are mainly three methods which are used to estimate the value of environmental quality. First, the value of, for example, visiting a recreational site, can be estimated from the travelling costs that people are prepared to pay to visit the site. Second, pollution and noise will affect values of real estate, and from estimating how such environmental differences affect the values of houses in different areas, we can estimate how people value these aspects of the environment. Both these methods are limited in application, since they can only measure the 'use-value' of the environment, that is, the value of the environment in use for recreation or inhabiting. Only the third method, the contingent valuation method (CVM), can possibly reveal the preferences for non-use aspects of the environment. For a presentation of CVM, see Mitchell and Carsson (1989). The CVM estimate of non-use values is controversial. Two objections are relevant to the discussion here, that is, embedding and pure altruism.

Economic valuation of environmental quality is described in many textbooks (see, for example, Mitchell and Carsson, 1989, Pearce and Warford, 1993 or Hanley and Spash, 1993). For a general discussion of the theory of cost–benefit analysis, see Drèze and Stern (1987) or Atkinson and Stiglitz (1980).

Economic valuation of environmental quality is based on the Samuelson–Bergson approach to welfare economics.[7] We found above that the difference in welfare at two states x and x^* can be approximated as:

$$W(x) - W(x^*) \approx \sum_{i=1}^{I} \frac{\partial V}{\partial U_i}(\sum_{n=1}^{N} \frac{\partial U_i}{\partial x_{in}}(x_{in} - x_{in}^*)) \qquad (5.6)$$

where N is the number of commodities, and x_{in} is consumer i's consumption of commodity n. Assuming utility maximization subject to

---

[7] The current presentation of valuation is the most relevant for the measurement of national welfare, but valuation is sometimes introduced without defining a welfare function. The alternative to using a welfare function is to identify potentially Pareto-improving projects, see below.

a budget equation, we further derived

$$\frac{\partial U_i / \partial x_{in}}{\partial U_i / \partial x_{ik}} = \frac{p_n}{p_k}.$$

For public goods, this equality is no longer true, since the amount of public goods a person consumes is not chosen to maximize his/her utility.

To simplify, consider the case with only two commodities, money and environmental quality. As above we assume that income is redistributed to maximize social welfare, so that each individual's consumption of good 1 contributes equally to social welfare. This means that an additional dollar contributes the same to social welfare irrespective of who gets it. We normalize so that

$$\frac{\partial V}{\partial U_i} \frac{\partial U_i}{\partial x_{i1}} = 1, \text{ for all } i. \tag{5.7}$$

With this normalization we derive

$$\frac{\partial V}{\partial U_i} \frac{\partial U_i}{\partial x_{i2}} = \frac{(\partial V / \partial U_i)(\partial U_i / \partial x_{i2})}{(\partial V / \partial U_i)(\partial U_i / \partial x_{i1})} - \frac{\partial U_i / \partial x_{i2}}{\partial U_i / \partial x_{i1}} - MWTP_i. \tag{5.8}$$

The last fraction is the marginal utility of environment to the marginal utility of income. This expresses how many units of income the person could give up for an additional unit of environmental quality, and still maintain utility, that is, the MWTP (marginal willingness to pay). Inserting (5.8) into (5.6) we get,

$$W(x) - W(x^*) \approx \sum_{i=1}^{I} (x_{i1} - x_{i1}^*) + \sum_{i=1}^{I} MWTP_i(x_2 - x_2^*), \tag{5.9}$$

where the first term on the right-hand side is the total income change and the last part is the total willingness to pay for the environmental changes. Thus if total willingness to pay for the move from x_2^* to x_2, exceeds the cost $\sum_{i=1}^{I}(x_{i1}^* - x_{i1})$, the state x gives higher social welfare than x^*. To reach this conclusion, we had to assume that a dollar extra to some individual contributes equally to social welfare, independent of who receives it. Since this assumption is not obviously reasonable, we next study the consequences of relaxing it.

5.7.1 Welfare Weights

In the analysis above we derived the condition that an extra dollar contributes equally to social welfare irrespective of who receives it, from an assumption that income is costlessly redistributed to maximize social welfare. This is not very reasonable; it is not costless to redistribute income, and the redistribution that does take place reflects not only attempts to maximize social welfare, but also the structure of power and influence in the society. Moreover, we have derived the social welfare function corresponding to an arbitrary person by considering his/her preferences as a benevolent dictator. Since these preferences depend on who makes the judgement, income cannot be redistributed to make marginal utility equal according to everybody's judgement.

To see the implications of income distribution not being optimal, we define the welfare weights $\beta_i = (\partial V/\partial U_i)(\partial U_i/\partial x_{i1})$. Now (5.9) becomes

$$W(x) - W(x^*) \approx \sum_{i=1}^{I} \beta_i \left[(x_{i1} - x_{i1}^*) + MWTP_i(x_2 - x_2^*) \right], \quad (5.10)$$

In Section 5.1 we saw that with an optimal income distribution, $\beta_i = (\partial V/\partial U_i)(\partial U_i/\partial x_{i1})$, would be equal for all i. Normalizing so that $\beta_i = 1$, we see that welfare weights will not count. Since income distribution is hardly optimal, this assumption is not reasonable. It is illuminating to consider the case where we assume that marginal utility of environmental quality is equal, instead of assuming equal marginal utility of money. Formally this would imply that all $(\partial V/\partial U_i)(\partial U_i/\partial x_2)$ are independent of i, instead of $(\partial V/\partial U_i)(\partial U_i/\partial x_{i1})$ being independent of i. We see from (5.10) that $(\partial V/\partial U_i)(\partial U_i/\partial x_2)$ would be independent of i if $\beta_i = 1/MWTP_i$.

To analyse the empirical importance of this issue, I used the data from a survey conducted by Strand (1985) in Brekke (1996). To make the result comparable with standard environmental valuation, consider the case that $(x_{i1} - x_{i1}^*)$ is equal for all i, which was approximately true in that particular example. I found that with 31 kroner lost income $((x_{i1} - x_{i1}^*) = -31$ kr) from a carbon tax that lowered emissions of the main pollutants to air by 50 per cent, the net benefits would just balance. This can be compared to the average willingness to pay in money terms of 685 kroner. The choice between $(\partial V/\partial U_i)(\partial U_i/\partial x_2)$ or $(\partial V/\partial U_i)(\partial U_i/\partial x_{i1})$ being independent of i, thus changes the value with a factor of 22.

Brekke (1996) shows that this choice corresponds to choosing either money $((\partial V/\partial U_i)(\partial U_i/\partial x_{i1})$ being equal) or environmental quality units $((\partial V/\partial U_i)(\partial U_i/\partial x_2)$ being equal) as numeraire, and that money as a numeraire favours those with high MWTP (referred to as the 'environmentalists'). The net benefit of the project for the environmentalist becomes a large number if expressed in money units since money is of low value to him/her. On the other hand, if the net benefit is expressed in environmental quality units, then the net benefit would be a small number, since environmental quality is important to the environmentalist. Similarly the net benefit for the 'materialist' (with low MWTP), is only a tiny number if expressed in money terms, but large in environmental quality units. Generally we would expect it would be favourable for a group if the good that is chosen as numeraire is one which they value less than other groups.

The crucial question then becomes: is there any reason to prefer one choice to the other? The main difference is if we let all welfare weights be equal, then, for any project that increases welfare, the winners can compensate the losers with monetary side payments.

The Hicks–Kaldor (Kaldor, 1939; Hicks, 1939) criterion for project evaluation claims that the project is preferable if the winners *poten-*

tially can compensate the losers. No compensation has to be paid. But if no compensation is actually paid, the criterion is not attractive. On the other hand, if compensation is paid, the concept of potential Pareto improvement is redundant since the project is a real Pareto improvement.

Perhaps the most compelling argument for the Hicks–Kaldor criterion is that many potential Pareto improvements make up something close to a real one. A discussion of this claim is given in Frank (1992, p. 160). He emphasizes that cost–benefit analysis should be evaluated as a general decision rule that is applied to a large number of projects, and that the distribution consequences of all the projects should be seen in connection with the possibility of redistribution throughout the tax system. He concludes that

> This search [for social choice mechanisms] has arisen out of a misguided focus on the effect of individual policy decisions and the impracticability of making compensations on a case-by-case basis. Once we focus on finding a general policy for making a large number of social decisions and recognize that compensation for general biases is possible through the tax system, it becomes clear that we have had a perfectly good social choice mechanism all along, namely the cost–benefit criterion.

Disregarding for the moment the possibility of using taxes to compensate for general biases, we first discuss the claim that when using the cost–benefit criterion for a large number of projects, everyone will be better off. The same argument was used by Edgeworth (1881) as an argument for utilitarianism. His argument was framed in terms of utility units and not monetary units. The argument works equally well for any choice of numeraire.

Unlike the case with utility or other numeraires, it is in principle possible to use taxes to compensate for general biases. Note, however, that in our discussion no assumptions have been made about income distribution. The side payments considered are a redistribution between individuals with *different taste*, not a redistribution between individuals with *different income*. The taxes that would be required to compensate for biases would then depend on a person's taste and not his/her income. For a further discussion, see Brekke (1996).

5.7.2 Embedding, Pure Altruism, Agency.

The discussion above on whether well-being should be seen as utility is also relevant here. When surveys are used to determine a person's willingness to pay (WTP), the person is asked to make hypothetical choices, and it is this choice behaviour that is used to determine the WTP. This approach therefore sees well-being as utility. The criticism to this view on well-being is thus also relevant here, and, as I interpret the discussion, this is the heart of the current controversy[8] over contingent valuation studies. Is the maximization of well-being really the sole motive for human choices?

One criticism is related to the maximization assumption as presented in Kahneman and Knetch (1992). They claimed that when people were asked to value an environmental good, they were not giving their preferences for pairs (x_i, E). Rather they have a mental account for good purposes, that is spent on the first good project they are presented with.[9] To support this claim empirically they conducted an experiment where they found that the WTP was rather unresponsive to the size of the environmental change ΔE, but very responsive to whether the project was presented as part of a larger project. Kahneman and Knetch's paper has stimulated much discussion. Smith (1993)

---

[8]This controversy was recently a topic in an issue of *Journal of Economic Perspectives*. See Hahnemann (1994), Portney (1994) and Diamond and Hausmann (1994).

[9]A similar idea has been introduced in the theory of private provision of public goods, where it is assumed that a private good 'charitable donation' is acquired simultaneously with a donation. This assumption is required to avoid a conclusion that taxes are neutral. See Andreoni (1990), Bernheim (1986), Olsson (1965), Sudgen (1984) and Cornes and Sandler (1994).

argued that their findings are not inconsistent with standard theory, while Diamond and Hausman (1994) claim that the findings would imply elasticities that are too large to be believable. Hahneman (1994) claims that the lack of sensitivity to ΔE is due to poor experimental design, and is not replicated in less casual studies.

Another objection to the CVM was raised by Milgrom (1993), with the question 'Is sympathy an economic value?'. He argued that when the stated WTP had altruistic motives, there arises the problem of double counting: 'counting one person's willingness to pay for another's happiness in a benefit–cost calculation amounts to a double (or triple or ...) counting of the beneficiary's preferences'. Johansson (1992, 1994) has formalized this claim and discusses potential solutions to it.

A related problem is whether altruism is an argument for not seeing well-being as utility. Remember the quotation above, with the two boys who found a cake. The boy who proposed an equal share, probably took the other boy's interest into account, and hence the other boy's interest was counted twice in the proposed compromise. Unless all agents are equally altruistic, the utilitarian calculus is adding incommensurable utilities. Sagoff (1988) argues that people's attitudes to environmental projects express their social values not their individual preferences, and that social values are shaped by public discussion and should not be aggregated.

The discussion about valuation of environmental quality, especially CVM, is still running. The proponents will hold that this is the best method available, while others argue that in this case no number is better than some number. For the measurement of welfare changes over time, this controversy adds to the already significant problems of intertemporal comparison of welfare.

5.8   HICKSIAN INCOME REVISITED

It will be recalled from Chapter 3 that Hicks's definition of income is the amount a person can spend during a week and still be as well off at the end of the week as in the beginning. In Chapter 3 we interpreted 'as well off' in terms of affluence, that is, as a requirement that it should be possible to maintain an equally large budget set in all future periods. An alternative interpretation of 'as well off' is in terms of welfare, that is, a requirement that the person should be able to maintain the welfare.

A welfare interpretation of 'as well off' in the definition of income, would have several advantages. In Chapter 3, we had no good solution to how to compare budget sets when relative prices are changing. With a welfare interpretation we could use price indexes for this purpose, as discussed above. Moreover, we can extend the definition to include the effects of environmental degradation.

The drawbacks are equally clear. Defining income by the use of welfare we encounter all the problems of measuring welfare, as discussed in the last chapter. In particular, the problem of intertemporal comparison of welfare is an important obstacle to this approach. I will demonstrate that even with an intertemporally comparable welfare concept, the income concept has some counterintuitive properties, especially if we accept that preferences are not intertemporally separable. The resulting income concept is hardly useful for practical purposes. Moreover, it will be difficult to maintain the distinction between a country's economic resources and what it achieves with these resources.

In Chapter 3, we defined the Hicksian income as maximal sustainable consumption, where sustainability was defined as non-declining consumption. Assuming that welfare is intertemporally comparable, the natural extension is weak sustainability, that utility is non-declining. With intertemporally separable preferences, and with consumption as a scalar, this would not make any difference, since $u(c_t) \leq u(c_{t+1})$ is equivalent to $c_t \leq c_{t+1}$, with u increasing. On the other hand, defining sustainability as non-decreasing welfare is much more general, since this gives a basis for handling changes in relative prices through price indexes. If preferences are intertemporally non-separable, however, the two definitions can become markedly different.

To see this definition at work with intertemporally non-separable utility, suppose that the utility is $u(c_t, c_{t-1}) = \sqrt{c_t - 0.9c_{t-1}}$. The parameters in this utility function are not based on empirical analysis but are chosen to illustrate the discussion. The consumption standard z_t is assumed to be last period's consumption c_{t-1}. Thus the person quickly gets accustomed to a new level of consumption.

Consider a small nation in an economy where prices and interest rates are constant over time. Assume that the person is spending a wealth of 100 with a constant interest rate equal to 10 per cent. This is Hicks's own example where he concluded that the income was 10. Now suppose that $c_0 = 1$, what, then, is the Hicksian income according to the definition above?

To see this, suppose we choose $c_1 = 3$. Can this be the first consumption level on a sustainable path? A sustainable path will be characterized by $u(c_t, c_{t-1}) \leq u(c_{t+1}, c_t)$ for all t. For such a path to be sustainable, we must thus maintain the utility $u(c_1, c_0) = \sqrt{2.1}$ for all future periods. Then we would have to choose c_2 such that $\sqrt{c_2 - 0.9 \cdot 3} = \sqrt{2.1}$. Thus $c_2 = 0.9 \cdot 3 + 2.1 = 4.8$. Similarly we get $c_3 = 0.9 \cdot 4.8 + 2.1 = 6.42$. Continuing this process, we find that $c_t \approx 21$ for t sufficiently large. The present value of this path is 119, and the path is infeasible with a wealth of 100. Thus, even $c_1 = 3$ is above the Hicksian income. According to the previous definition, the 'Hicksian income' turns out to be approximately[10] 2.65.

Even though we found that the income was approximately 2.65, it is true that a yearly consumption of 10 for all years is feasible. Nevertheless, with the given utility function, utility will be declining if we are consuming 10 every year. Though Hicks is among the critics of the intertemporal separability assumption, he takes for granted that if we can spend 10 every year with constant prices, the income is 10.

The conclusion that income in this particular case should be less than 10, appears to be counterintuitive. Perhaps my intuition is shaped

---

[10]This estimate obviously depends on the arbitrarily chosen parameters, and can be closer to 10 with other choices. Still, the example illustrates that income with this definition may deviate significantly from 10 with non-separable preferences.

by the idea of intertemporally separable preferences, but I still think that Hicksian income should not be based on a welfare interpretation of 'equally well off'. This conclusion is reinforced by the fact that I have disregarded the most important problem with a welfare-based definition of income: that we do not know how to measure intertemporally comparable welfare.

5.9 PRIMARY GOODS AND FUNCTIONINGS

If we have to give up the Bergson–Samuelson orthodoxy, what should be used instead? Perhaps the most important challenge to the orthodox position is the existence of theories, such as those of Rawls (1971) and Nozik (1974), which are not based on the concepts of utility. Are these alternatives relevant for our purpose where we want to reflect the national welfare consequences of environmental degradation? In some theories there are even no reason for welfare measures. For a discussion of how alternative moral philosophies relate to economic theory, see Hausman and McPherson (1996). Here, we shall consider only Rawls's philosophy and extensions of it.

Rawls (1971) introduces the concept of 'primary goods' as 'a simplification for the basis of interpersonal comparisons' (p. 92). Primary goods are 'things which it is supposed a rational man wants whatever else he wants'. Among the primary goods Rawls mentions 'rights and liberties, powers and opportunities, income and wealth, self respect, health and vigor, intelligence and imagination'.

Looking at the list of primary goods, we note that there is no direct reference to the natural environment. However, the environment fits well into the general idea of a primary good. Everybody wants clean air, whatever else they may want. Thus it seems natural to include a good environment in the list of primary goods.

Rawls talks about primary goods for each individual, to simplify interpersonal comparison as a basis for a discussion of what constitutes a just distribution. To use this concept to develop an alternative to a measure of national welfare is quite another issue. The income for a whole nation is an aggregate, suppressing considerable problems of interpersonal comparability. The approach thus seems to require that both level and distribution of primary goods are measured. Obviously, this will not give a definite ranking of nations or of states in different years, but may serve as a basis for a subjective judgement about such a ranking. After all, we argued above that the ranking of social states depends on who makes the judgement.

Even if everybody wants more income or wealth, whatever else they may want, it will be true that what you can achieve from your income, depends on other characteristics. Sen (1985a) introduced the concept of 'functionings' to cope with the differences in individual need for primary goods. For example, the nutritional needs of a person will depend upon characteristics of the person, such as weight and health (absence of parasitic diseases). Rawls' primary goods will reflect a person's resources while the functionings are closer to achievements. To reflect opportunity, Sen introduces 'capabilities' as the set of functionings a person can feasibly achieve.

As with Rawls, the aim is to develop a framework to discuss principal questions: should we strive for equality in terms of functionings or capabilities, rather than primary goods? Nevertheless, Sen's conceptual framework is much closer to traditional economic welfare theory. He argues that we, at least to some extent, will share the valuation of functionings. Thus if we can determine the relevant functionings derived from environmental services, and get an estimate of a common valuation of the functionings, then we have the basic ingredients for a welfare function. On the other hand, much more research is needed before this is an operational approach.

5.10   CONCLUSIONS

In the previous section I argued that there are good reasons to be sceptical of the possibility of measuring welfare. First, the orthodox position of traditional welfare economics, as represented by the Samuelson–Bergson welfare function, is subject to discussion. Second, the ranking of social states depends on who makes the judgement, primarily because no operational methods exist for interpersonal comparison of welfare. Third, important problems arise in attempting to compare welfare at different points in time and between different countries. Fourth, while the methods of valuation of environmental goods have developed considerably the last decade, there is currently much controversy about these methods. The problems with valuing environmental goods are no less when the purpose is the measurement of national welfare.

To be sceptical is not to be critical, and if required it may be wise to go for an imperfect solution rather than no solution. Whether the objections that are raised above are so serious that we should give up adjusting GDP to measure welfare, depends on the purpose of the measurement. I think that the primary objective of improving the informational basis for environmental policy, is not to measure welfare, or to correct the national accounting measures. The primary objective should rather be to make sure that all the relevant aspects of the development are properly taken into account in the political decision process.

To make sure that environmental concerns are properly taken into account in the decision making, would not require a national welfare indicator. We should give higher priority to collecting the required information and present it in a way that is generally understood. It is also important to integrate environmental issues into economic models to allow us to assess the environmental impact of the environmental policy.

The questions which remain and which a national welfare measure would help to answer are exactly those where I have argued that the current measures face most problems: the intertemporal and international comparison of welfare.

Many welfare measures which include environmental quality have been proposed. In the next chapter we will consider some of these.

The objective is not to be comprehensive, and many proposals will not be commented upon. Rather, the objective to demonstrate the variety of different proposals and to discuss how the main ideas relate to the discussion in this chapter. I will argue that many of the proposals that have been put forward as improvements of GDP as a welfare measure could better be considered as improvements to GDP as a measure of the economic determinant of welfare: that is, income.

6. Environmental Degradation

In Chapters 3 and 4, when we discussed the measurement of national income, the resource and environmental issues were restricted to purely commercial resources. This is clearly a very strong limitation that excludes many important environmental changes that have run alongside economic growth. To be true, there is hardly any purely commercial resource, in the sense that the extraction and use of most resources has an impact on the environment.

Most cases of environmental degradation will have some impact on marketable goods. Loss of biodiversity will limit the possibility of discovering new medicines. Polluted air may affect the health of the labour stock and thus the efficiency of labour may decrease and wages will decrease too. Fishing permits would be valueless if the lake no longer supported life. Nevertheless, market prices do not capture all the negative effects of environmental degradation. Polluted air can have a considerable effect on the welfare of individuals in a society, even when the effect on wages is very small. Clearly, a measure based purely on market prices cannot fully reflect environmental changes. Perhaps the most important changes are those that are not reflected by market prices.

The limited inclusion of environmental issues in Chapter 3 and 4 was in part due to the focus on income measurement. I will argue in this chapter that the income concept can be extended to deal with restrictions on environmental degradation, but the reason for putting up such restrictions in the first place is usually that environmental degradation affects welfare. Having discussed the measurement of welfare, we are thus ready to consider how to account for environmental degradation.

In this chapter we will examine some of the main proposals for correcting GDP for account for environmental degradation. For most, although not all, proposals the purpose of the proposed adjustments is to get a better measure of welfare, but I will argue that some of them are better seen as adjustments required to measure income.

6.1   SUBTRACTING DEFENSIVE EXPENDITURES

The idea of subtracting defensive expenditures is due to Nordhaus and Tobin (1972), who called them 'instrumental expenditures'. Their expressed intention, by subtracting these expenditures, is to get a better measure of what they call 'economic welfare' or 'true consumption'. They use national defence as an example: 'Has the value of the nation's security risen from $0.5 billion to $50 billion over the period from 1929 to 1965? Obviously not'. It is claimed that defence expenditures have no direct effect on household economic welfare and that these expenses are input rather than output.

Nordhaus and Tobin (1972, p. 7) introduced 'Instrumental' or 'defensive' expenditures by arguing that 'many activities ... are evidently not directly sources of utility themselves but are regrettably necessary inputs to activities that may yield utility'. Similarly Daly and Cobb (1990, p. 71) argue that 'Defensive expenditures are of the nature of intermediate goods; that is, they are cost of production rather than final products available for consumption'. Likewise, Eisner (1988, p. 1617) states: 'We focus on the final product, those goods and services that are the penultimate ingredients of human well-being, and try to avoid double counting by separating out the intermediate product, which constitutes a cost, possibly a varying cost, of producing the final output with which we are concerned'.

Unfortunately, the distinction between inputs and products for final consumption is not clear. In Becker's (1976) model of household production, most consumption goods are treated as input in the household production function. Similarly, Sen (1985a) makes a distinction between the commodities, their characteristics and the functionings they provide. In this setup, the functionings and not the commodities are the objects of valuation. We do not consume clothes as such, but the services they provide, such as keeping us warm and allowing us to appear in public without embarrassment. So why exclude some expenses and not all?

To analyse these points, consider the following very simple model where the utility, $u(c, s)$, depends on the level of consumption, c, and the level of some service, s, in the society. $u(c, s)$ is the instantaneous welfare of a representative individual and the utility function u is assumed to be unchanged over time. Assuming a representative individual, we disregard for the moment many of the problems with welfare measurement which were discussed above.

The amount of services enjoyed depends on the amount of defensive expenditures d used as inputs in the production of services, represented by the production function $s = f(d, \theta)$ where f_d is strictly positive, but decreasing in d. (Subscripts denote partial derivatives.) θ may reflect dependence on developments that are exogenous in this model, such as the level of urbanization or specialization of production. Total production y must be allocated to either consumption or defensive expenditures, $y = c + d$.

As a linear approximation, dividing through with marginal utility u_c, changes in utility can be written

$$\frac{\Delta u}{u_c} = \Delta c + \frac{u_s}{u_c} \Delta s = \Delta y - \Delta d + \frac{u_s}{u_c} \Delta s. \tag{6.1}$$

Alternatively, inserting for $s = f(d, \theta)$ in the utility function, we find the approximation

$$\Delta u = u_c \Delta c + u_s (f_d \Delta d + f_\theta \Delta \theta).$$

Assuming that d and c are chosen to maximize utility $u(c, f(d, \theta))$ subject to the budget constraint $c + d = y$, we get first-order condition

$f'_d u_s = u_c$. Inserting into the expression above, we find that

$$\frac{\Delta u}{u_c} = \Delta c + \Delta d + \frac{u_s}{u_c} f_\theta \Delta \theta = \Delta y + \frac{u_s}{u_c} f_\theta \Delta \theta. \tag{6.2}$$

This shows that there are two ways of reporting the welfare changes, either subtracting defensive expenditures and adding the effect of changes in level of s as in (6.1), or including defensive expenditures and adding the effect of changes in external factors (6.2). In both cases, adjustments require that the shadow price on the service, u_s/u_c, are known.

Whether or not it is preferable to include defensive expenditures depends on the kind of information that is available. If we know $f_\theta \Delta \theta$, especially if $\Delta \theta = 0$, we should include the defensive expenditures, while if $f_\theta \Delta \theta$ is unknown, it may be easier to exclude the defensive expenditures and try to estimate $u_s \Delta s$. For a further discussion, see Brekke and Gravningsmyhr (1994), on which parts of this and the next section is based.

In a comment on Nordhaus and Tobin's work, Jaszi (1973) argued that the list of defensive expenditures could be extended to include almost anything. Food, for example, is an intermediate good, used to provide nutrition and assuage hunger. Food expenses are defensive against hunger and could be discarded. Daly and Cobb (1990, p. 78) respond to this criticism that defensive expenditures are 'defense against unwanted side effects of other production, not a defense against normal baseline environmental conditions like cold, rain and so on'. They do not offer any explanation of why this distinction is important to welfare measures, but the term 'baseline environmental conditions' indicates that they think of conditions that are constant over time, hence $\Delta \theta = 0$.

Provided basic needs are constant, Daly and Cobb (1990) would be correct in claiming that expenditures that are defensive against hunger, should not be subtracted. It may be argued that even basic needs may change: the nutritional needs of an academic professor are probably on average less than those of a person doing heavy manual labour, and the share of labour force in the different occupations changes over time. Nevertheless, assuming constant basic needs may be the least problematic assumption we will have to make.

A more important problem is that, as pointed out in the previous chapter, relative consumption matters for both psychological and practical reasons. Let s denote the ability to participate in social life, or the ability to use possessions to communicate membership of a specific class. These services are clearly affected by social parameters that are not constant over time. Increased consumption of observable commodities may be required just to 'keep up with the Joneses'. These extra consumption expenses are thus defensive against a possible decline in social standing. The list of expenditures which are defensive in this sense, would include a large share of private consumption; not a very tempting conclusion.

6.1.1 Economic Welfare as Income

Nordhaus and Tobin (1972) intended to improve GDP as a measure of 'economic welfare'. The term 'economic welfare' is also used in similar adjustments in the same tradition. As discussed in Chapter 5, it is not straightforward to separate different parts of welfare. The kind of adjustment suggested, however, makes it reasonable to interpret the term as 'income', perhaps in a wide sense.

In Chapter 3 we tried to keep a distinction between the resources available and the welfare derived from these resources, and we interpreted the income as an estimate of the resources available. This idea is similar to Eisner's (1988, p. 1617) claim that the account should 'measure not the welfare itself but the production of final good and services which are presumed to contribute to welfare'. The problem is in either case to identify the 'final goods and services'. If we focus on functionings, as in Sen (1985) two persons will have equal resources if their capabilities are equal. Since participating in social life is a functioning, the expenses for 'keeping up with the Joneses' would be defensive expenditures required to maintain the capability to participate in social life. Nevertheless, I think there are good reason for not treating the expenditures required to maintain social standing as defensive.

First, from a pragmatic point of view, changes in the amount, or quality, of intangible goods are hard to measure. How do we estimate changes in national security or the expenses needed to participate in social life, or to maintain self-respect? Estimates of these quantities would to a large extent have to be based on subjective judgements. It is thus preferable to base measures on more tangible final goods and services. Nevertheless, to define final goods for practical purposes, many choices remain, (see Eisner, 1988 for a discussion).

Having determined the final good, how should we measure income? In Chapter 3, income was defined as the maximum sustainable consumption. Extending the focus beyond market commodities, a possible extension would be to require that not only per capita consumption is constant, but also other services such as environmental quality. As above, we would not extend the constancy to intangibles, but not all non-marketed services are intangible. In many cases the service s_t may be expressed in physical units, for example, the concentration of pollutants in the air.

Let $\bar{d}(\theta_t)$ be the amount required to keep the services at some given level constant, $s_t = \bar{s}$. That is, $\bar{d}$ is implicitly defined by $f(\bar{d}(\theta), \theta) = \bar{s}$. Now, $y_t - c_t$ is the amount that can be used for the consumption of commercial goods, given the restriction that $s_t = \bar{s}$. The parameter θ_t has been exogenous, but for many applications it would be reasonable to let $\theta_t = s_{t-1}$. For example, we may assume that the cost of achieving a level of the environmental services $\bar{s}$, would depend on the state of the environment we inherited. Thus, along a path with s constant, θ will be constant.

Let y_t be the Hicksian income when the service s_t is not taken into account. Now $y_t - \bar{d}(\theta_t)$ would be the natural extension of Hicksian income to account for the service s. Since y_t is Hicksian income, the nation can continue to spend that amount on the supply of the service and commercial goods, for ever. Since θ_t is constant, the nation can also maintain the consumption of commercial goods and the level of s forever.

The approach may also be extended to the case where θ_t is not expected to remain constant. Suppose that θ_s for $s \geq t$ is known. To keep $s_s = \bar{s}$ now takes a stream of defensive expenditures $\bar{d}(\theta_s)$. The part of the total wealth that is left for ordinary consumption is total wealth less the present value of the defensive expenditures. Hence the Hicksian income is

$$c_t = \frac{r}{1+r} \left[W_t - \sum_{s=t}^{\infty} \bar{d}(\theta_s)(1+r)^{-(s-t)} \right].$$

If $\bar{d}(\theta_s)$ is constant, the Hicksian income is $(r/(1+r))W_t - \bar{d}(\theta_t)$. The Hicksian income will be less than $(r/(1+r))W_t - \bar{d}(\theta_t)$ if the defensive expenditures have to increase to keep s constant. In the era of the arms race, extracting only the current defence expenses was perhaps too optimistic?

Note that the income interpretation is independent of the preferences, it is based only on an investigation of the feasible set, that is, how much it is feasible to consume, subject to the constraint that $s_t = \bar{s}$. Social processes may affect what we get out of the income or how we perceive the environmental status, but those processes are independent of the discussion on how to measure income.

6.2 DISAMENITIES OF URBANIZATION

From 1950 to 1985 the share of the world population living in urban areas increased from 29 per cent to 41 per cent (WCED, 1987). If the income in urban areas are higher than in rural areas, this migration may be a significant contribution to economic growth, since GDP will increase as a person moves to a better paid job. On the other hand, if people would, other things being equal, prefer to live in rural areas, we may overestimate the growth. A person will move to a city if the wage difference exceeds the disamenity of moving. If he/she is indifferent about moving to an urban area or staying in the rural area, he/she has no welfare gain from moving. Nevertheless, the wage difference may be positive, and contribute to the GDP growth. For this reason, Nordhaus and Tobin (1972) suggested that growth rates should be adjusted for urbanization.

This adjustment of GDP will not be consistent with the interpretation of the measure of economic welfare as income, nor will it be consistent with Eisner's (1988) interpretation as ' ... the goods and services ... contributing to welfare'. Nordhaus and Tobin are rather trying to measure welfare itself, and all the comments on welfare measurement from Chapter 5 apply. I will not repeat those arguments here, but rather focus on those issues that are specific to this model.

Nordhaus and Tobin noted that when GDP is used as a measure of welfare, migration from rural into urban areas will show up as an increase in welfare because of the higher income in the cities (assuming that income is higher in urban than in rural areas): 'some portion of the higher earnings of the urban residents may simply be compensation for the disamenities of urban life and work'.[1] This means that GDP does not necessarily represent the welfare effects of migration correctly.

Nordhaus and Tobin (1972) estimated these disamenities from migration data, and we will return to that approach below. First we consider the approach in Daly and Cobb (1990), who estimated the disamenity by identifying some of its components, and valued each of them separately. Their adjustments for urbanization included three elements, cost of commuting, cost of housing and disutility from externalities. The first two may be considered defensive expenditures. Commuting to and from work is a service that is necessary in order to get to work, and the cost of commuting changes due to external forces

---

[1]Nordaus and Tobin (1972), p. 13.

such as increased urbanization. That is, the service 'getting to work' is the same at all locations and at all points in time and $\Delta s = 0$, and hence we should, according to the analysis in Section 6.1, subtract the cost of commuting. If there are systematic differences in costs of commuting between urban and rural areas, this would change the measured welfare improvements from migration, which is the reason for correcting for disamenities of urbanization.

A similar argument applies to the cost of housing. Because of higher population densities in urban areas, land prices will be higher in urban areas. This implies higher costs of buying or renting a house or apartment. Urbanization will add to growth if the income is higher in urban areas, but the extra cost of commuting and housing will not be deducted.

Finally, Daly and Cobb estimated the value of negative urban externalities. Inhabitants in urban areas experience a higher level of pollution, violence and so on, which can be expected to yield disutility. Daly and Cobb's (1990) estimate of the disamenity of urbanization is based on an assumption that the welfare effects of living in urban areas (apart from higher wages) are negative. The positive externalities of urban life like more variety of available jobs, easy access to cultural and social events, and less stringent social control, are completely ignored. There are people (like Woody Allen's characters) who prefer the urban way of life and perhaps are even willing to pay for it.[2] Perhaps the high costs of living in urban areas may just reflect the size of these positive externalities? If these positive externalities are large, the adjustments made by Daly and Cobb may even be in the wrong direction.

6.2.1 Rural–urban Migration

Nordhaus and Tobin (1972) suggested that disamenities should be estimated on the basis of observed choices between urban and rural life,

---

[2]See Berman (1982) and Sennet (1990) for a discussion of the role of the cities and the urban influence on man, society and the arts.

through migration data. Their empirical results support the hypothesis that the negative externalities outweigh the positive ones, as they found a positive disamenity of urbanization, based on migration data.

In Norway it was difficult to get some groups such as teachers, medical doctors and police officers, to work in the northern rural areas. The wages for these groups were the same all over the country, and the cost of living is lower in the rural areas. The problem has been amended by introducing extra bonuses and other advantages for those who are willing to work in the northern rural areas. These observations indicate that the positive externalities may well outweigh the negative ones.

Both observations have their shortcomings. Nordhaus and Tobin's (1972) analysis implicitly assumed that migration is caused by the wage difference between urban and rural areas, corrected for the willingness to pay for living in rural areas. This is an elegant but simple model of migration, and many important factors are left out. For example, there are important links between migration and both fertility and education. Moreover, the migrants, external effects on others, for example, through more congestion on the highways, are not accounted for.

Nordhaus and Tobin's data only gave the migration rates for different areas without information on whether the migration was from rural to urban areas, while the main share of migration in the United States is between urban areas. The Norwegian observations on the other hand, are rather limited, for example, the cost of moving is not accounted for. Moreover, the Nordic climate is cold and it is dark all day during winter, and hence the urban–rural dimension is not the whole story of this migration.[3] For a discussion, see Brekke and Gravningsmyhr (1994).

The two observations may not be inconsistent. Incentives to settle in rural areas are intended to move people accustomed to an urban life, and they may prefer the urban life. Those migrating from rural areas on the other hand, may prefer the rural life. Tendencies to habit formation

---

[3]Should it count as positive in a welfare measure when people move from an unpleasant to a more pleasant climate?

and adjustments will also pose problems for the interpretation of the migratory data. It may take a positive income gap to make people move to an urban area, and a positive gap to make them move back.

Assuming rationality and perfect foresight, a person moving to an urban area will take into account the fact that the disamenity will change over time, and will judge the present value of income differences against the present value of the disamenities. If that is the case, then migration data can be used to estimate the disamenities. On the other hand, studies by Kahneman and Varey (1992) indicate that people are unable to predict how their preferences will change.

The discussion shows that the adjustment could be both positive and negative, and that it is not clear from migratory data wheter the dominating externalities are negatives, which are the only ones accounted for in Daly and Cobb (1990).

To use migratory data to estimate the disamenity of urbanization, we must also take care to avoid double counting. The extra pollution in urban areas is a part of the externality used to explain migration. Part of the disamenity of pollution will thus be accounted for in migratory data, and should not be counted again in a measure of the value of environmental degradation.

Note, finally, that the discussion is related to migration in industrialized countries while urbanization is at least as important in developing countries. For a discussion of rural–urban migration in developing countries, see Stark (1991).

6.3   SUSTAINABLE ENVIRONMENTAL STANDARDS

If defensive expenditures are the expenditures required to maintain a service at a certain level $\bar{s}$, then we can extend that idea to set a target for s that is different from some historical level. Roefie Hueting suggests that $\bar{s}$ should be set to a 'sustainable environmental standard'.

Hueting (1989) considers three alternative corrections of GDP. First by subtracting actual environmental outlays. He criticizes this approach mainly on the grounds that much environmental degradation is not restored, and hence the real damage is not reflected in outlays. In terms of the notation in Section 6.1, $\Delta s \neq 0$. He also considers the possibility of 'correcting for defensive expenditures through surveys', by using data on willingness to pay. Being critical of the valuation studies, he also rejects this approach.

His proposal is to use 'standards for sustainable economic development' to correct for the defensive expenditures. In Hueting's (1989, p. 35) own words the idea is 'supplementing the correction for defensive environmental outlays with estimates of the expenditure on the measures required to meet physical standards for the availability and quality of environmental functions'.

The term 'environmental functions' is in some respects similar to Sen's concept of 'functionings', discussed in Chapter 5. For example, functions related to surface and ground water include 'water for drinking, for agriculture, for cooling, for fishing' and so on (Hueting, 1989, p. 35). Central to Hueting's suggestion is the assumption that we can identify certain levels of these functions, 'the standard for sustainable use' that are required for sustainability.

An essential component of Hueting's argument is a supply or cost curve. The curve is drawn in Figure 6.1, taken from Hueting, Bosh and de Boer (1992). In Figure 6.1, A is the availability of functions in the year of investigation and S is the 'standard of sustainable use'. The distance from A to S must be bridged to arrive at the sustainable use of environmental functions. The distance from B to C is defined as the minimum cost that must be incurred to bridge the distance between the present situation and the sustainable use of the environment.

To present this idea with our notation, we extend the cost of maintaining a specific level of services $s_t = \bar{s}$, represented by the function $\bar{d}(\theta_t)$ in Section 6.2. We now need to refer to the yearly cost to implement any path $s_1, s_2, s_3, \ldots$. Let $\bar{s}$ correspond to the standard of sustainable use, and let $\hat{s}_0, \hat{s}_1, \hat{s}_2, \ldots$, be a path that converges to $\bar{s}$. To implement this path takes a stream of defensive expenditures, where

Figure 6.1 Hueting's transition cost

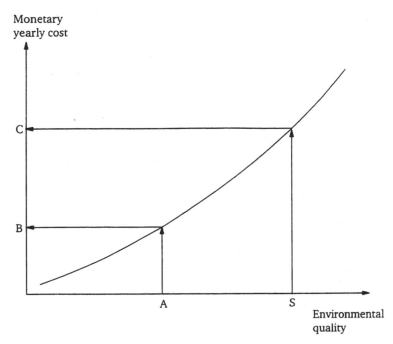

Source: Hueting, Bosh and de Boer (1992), p. 4.

the expenditures at time t depends on the change in state at that time, and are denoted $d(\hat{s}_t, \hat{s}_{t-1})$. Just as in Section 6.1, we should subtract the present value of this stream from the wealth to find what is left for ordinary consumption.

The standard of sustainable use is essential to Hueting's proposal. At the outset it is not obvious that this standard is uniquely defined, rather we would expect that there should be a trade-off between the level of environmental functions, and material consumption. A waterfall of scenic beauty may be kept for its aesthetic value or used for hydroelectric power generation. Which of these options are chosen will have an impact both on energy prices and on the availability of environmental functions in the long run. On the other hand, both of them may be consistent with sustainable development. Why, then, is there a unique level of availability of environmental functions, labelled the standard of environmental use?

Note, however, that Hueting is not the only one to suggest the use of such standards. The definition of 'strong sustainability' builds on a similar idea of keeping the environmental quality at a constant level, and not accepting other goods as substitutes for environmental quality, (see Page 1983). Randall and Farmer (1995) argue that cost-benefit analyses should be supplemented with restrictions to stay above 'safe minimum standards'. Many countries have in essence created standards through political decisions. National parks, national political aims for the emission of pollutants, or international environmental agreements, all in some sense set an environmental standard. If science cannot produce a unique environmental standard, we can still choose one.

Hueting does not claim to measure welfare or income, just to estimate what GDP would have been if we had implemented the standard. Hueting (1989, p. 32) gives impetus to his discussion with the claim that 'The misconception of terms reflect the belief that things go well, economically speaking, solely when production, as measured by gross domestic product (GDP), increases'. His suggestions bear some resemblance to the idea of defensive expenditures, and he considers his proposal as one of subtracting defensive expenditures. As discussed above, a welfare interpretation of such a subtraction requires that the services provided are constant, but Hueting also argues that the availability of environmental functions should not be constant, rather improved from A to S as in Figure 6.1.

We noted above that defensive expenditures can be interpreted as an adjustment to get a better measure of income, not welfare, and the approach could be generalized to the case of non-constant services s_t. While Hueting does not intend to measure income, it is interesting to generalize the income definition to the Hueting case. The idea is that if we accept that there is a unique standard of sustainable use, and that the availability of environmental functions s_t must be restored to this level in the long run, then the expenses incurred on this restoration will not be available for consumption.

Even if there is a unique sustainable environmental standard that is currently exceeded, as indicated in Figure 6.1, and which can be restored, the path of restoration may not be unique. If we close the gap from A to S in 10 years, the cost in the first year would be far less than the cost of closing the gap in one year.

The cost of this restoration would be a mixture of investment and maintenance. Consider the estimation of income for an open economy, and suppose that the availability of environmental functions is immediately restored to the standard of sustainable use at a cost c. The amount c can be borrowed from abroad at an interest rate r. The yearly cost of this investment will then be rc. Suppose, also, that maintaining the availability of environmental functions at the level S gives extra yearly production cost, m, compared to the level A. The present value of these costs is $c + m((1 + r)/r)$.

Now suppose that the restoration is delayed for T years. The current value of the costs is then $(c + m((1 + r)/r))(1 + r)^{-T}$. With $r = 5$ per cent, and with $T = 50$ years, the yearly costs are reduced by more than 90 per cent. Thus the approach not only requires that the standard of sustainable use, $\bar{s}$, is unique, but also that the path of restoration must be unique.

To summarize, we can compute the Hicksian income under the restriction that environmental quality should develop along some specific path. The corresponding adjustment will be different from that proposed by Hueting, who does not claim to measure income, since only the interest payment on the present value of the restoration cost would be subtracted. Moreover, the income would be very sensitive not only to the sustainable standard, but also to the path along which this standard is reached.

6.4   SYSTEM FOR INTEGRATED ENVIRONMENTAL AND ECONOMIC ACCOUNTING (SEEA)

In a Handbook of National Accounting (United Nations, 1993), a satellite System of Integrated Environmental and Economic Accounts (SEEA) has been developed to compute 'environmentally-adjusted net domestic product, EDP'. The EDP is presented in three different versions. The principles of these adjustments are later elaborated in Bartelmus and van Tongeren (1994), who state that

> One version applies a market valuation approach which rearranges only environmental changes already contained in the asset account in the conventional SNA. A second version uses a maintenance valuation which estimates the costs that would have been required to keep the natural environment intact during the accounting period. The third version combines the market valuation version with a contingent valuation approach in order to assess the environmental costs borne by industries with those borne by the household (as welfare losses from environmental deterioration). (p. 10)

The first version, affects only the assets, and thus not the measures of income and welfare. The second and third versions can be interpreted using the model in Section 6.2. Remember that the welfare changes are,

$$\frac{\Delta u}{u_c} = \Delta c + \frac{u_s}{u_c}\Delta s$$

where c is consumption and s in this context is the services from the environment. Total production is used for either consumption c or expenditures to increase the environmental services. The second version of SEEA can be interpreted as an estimate of what c would have been if defensive expenditures had been chosen so that $\Delta s = 0$. We argued above that this could, under some assumptions, be interpreted as income.

The third version would attempt a direct evaluation of the changes in environmental quality, the term $\Delta s \, u_s/u_c$. There are several advantages with this last version compared to the adjustments of income discussed above. First, the ambiguity of the environmental standard is removed. In addition, the method can evaluate any changes in s whether they apply to some standard or not. The problems with the approach are equally obvious, since valuation of environmental quality is required, with all the attendant problems as discussed in Chapter 5. The contingent valuation method is controversial, and, in the context of national welfare measures, there are additional problems with intertemporal and international comparisons.

6.5 NET NATIONAL PRODUCT AS A WELFARE MEASURE

In Chapter 4, we discussed the use of net national product as a measure of Hicksian income, or rather the connection between sustainability and net investment. In much of the literature the focus is, however, on measures of welfare. The interpretation of NNP (NNI in SNA, 1993) as a welfare measure was based on a result by Weitzman (1976), but in a generalized form, based on Mäler (1991). To present the main ideas of this approach, consider the following simplified version of Mäler's model.

Suppose that utility depends on consumption c_t and pollution x_t, $u(c_t, x_t)$. The utility is increasing in consumption and decreasing in pollution. The production function is $f(k_t, x_t)$, where k_t is capital, $f_k > 0$, and $f_x > 0$. With a constant utility discount rate, the problem is to maximize

$$\int_0^\infty u(c_t, x_t)e^{-\delta t}dt, \tag{6.3}$$

subject to $\dot{k}_t = f(k_t, x_t) - c_t$.

The Hamiltonian of this problem can be written as

$$H_t = u(c_t, x_t) + p_t^* \dot{k}_t$$
$$\approx u(c_t^*, x_t^*) + u_c \cdot (c_t - c_t^*) + u_x \cdot (x_t - x_t^*) + p_t^* \dot{k}_t,$$

where p_t^* is the shadow price of capital at the optimum. The stars denote the optimal path. The first-order condition for optimal consumption implies that $p_t^* = u_c$. Collecting all the stars, into a term denoted $\bar{H}_t$, and dividing through with $u_c(c_t^*, x_t^*)$, we get

$$\frac{H_t}{u_c} = \frac{\bar{H}_t}{u_c} + c_t + \dot{k}_t + \frac{u_x}{u_c} x_t. \tag{6.4}$$

The optimal policy is the one that maximizes the Hamiltonian, and this is also the policy that maximizes the linear approximation around the optimum, that is, it is optimal to maximize the right-hand side of (6.4) subject to the feasibility constraint, $c_t + \dot{k}_t = f(k_t, x_t)$. Since $\bar{H}_t/u_c$ is independent of c_t, x_t and $\dot{k}_t$, this is equivalent to maximizing the last three terms of (6.4).

As demonstrated in Chapter 4, with a constant discount rate, the Hamiltonian is proportional to the present value of future utility,

$$H_t^* = r \int_t^\infty u(c_s^*, x_s^*) e^{-\delta(s-t)} ds. \tag{6.5}$$

Mäler thus considers H_t^* as a welfare measure, and extends this interpretation to the linear approximation of H_t. In our particular model, his welfare measure, 'net national welfare measure, NWM', is defined by Mäler to be the last terms of (6.4),

$$NWM_t = c_t + \dot{k}_t + \frac{u_x}{u_c} x_t. \tag{6.6}$$

The first two terms of the NWM, consumption plus net investments, are the net national income, NNI. The NWM is thus an adjustment of NNI, where the direct benefits from pollution, $x_t u_x/u_c$, are added. (These 'benefits' are negative since $u_x < 0$.)

As pointed out in Chapter 4, this kind of model requires some form of constancy, and in this particular case it is required that the utility discount rate is constant. In Chapter 5 we argued that the intertemporal preference structure in (6.3) is not reasonable, because of individual and social habit formation. The model is, however, easily extended to cope with habit formation in preferences. To keep things simple we disregard pollution and environmental quality. Thus the problem is to maximize

$$\int_t^\infty u(c_s, z_s)e^{-\delta(s-t)}ds$$

where z_t is the consumption standard, which is increases when consumption is above the standard: $\dot{z}_t = \gamma(c_t - z_t)$. This is the formulation due to Ryder and Heal (1973). The capital accumulation is $\dot{k}_t = f(k_t) - c_t$, where k_t is capital. Equation (6.5) will still hold, but now the Hamiltonian is,

$$H_t = u(c_t, z_t) + p_t\dot{k}_t - \mu_t\dot{z}_t.$$

Linearizing this Hamiltonian gives

$$NWM_t = c_t + \dot{k}_t - \frac{\mu_t}{u_c}\dot{z}_t.$$

Note that we have not linearized with respect to z_t, since the consumption standard at time t is exogenously given and not influenced by the decision variable c_t. We conclude that NWM should also adjust for the negative impact of an increased consumption standard. In this model z_t is like a negative social capital, and the interpretation of the result above is that changes in this stock should be treated as investments.

As in Chapter 4, we can conclude that $u(c_t, z_t)$ cannot be non-declining if net investment $\dot{k}_t - \dot{z}_t\mu_t/u_c$ is negative, but in this case it does not follow that consumption is non-sustainable. Positive net investment, including a negative contribution from investment in consumption standard, is thus not a necessary condition for sustainability, interpreted as non-declining consumption.

The NWM is defined as the quantity that should be maximized at time t. To prove this, the Hamiltonian should be linearized *around the optimum*. This approximation is good only when the current policy is sufficiently close to the optimum and the prices that are used must be the optimum prices. It is not straightforward to estimate these prices?

One possibility is to construct a model of the economy, and solve it for the optimum. Then we would not need the linear approximation, since we are able to solve the non-linear model. An alternative is to assume that the economy is at the optimum, and use observed prices, as national accounts do. In this case we would find the right expression to maximize, but there is no need to maximize since the economy is at the optimum.

While NWM is constructed to compare welfare with different policies at time t, it is interesting to investigate whether NWM will also correctly report welfare changes over time. The question, in other words, is whether $NWM_t > NWM_{t'}$ implies that

$$\int_t^\infty u(c_s^*, x_s^*)e^{-\delta(s-t)}ds > \int_{t'}^\infty u(c_s^*, x_s^*)e^{-\delta(s-t')}ds.$$

Note first that this perspective on intertemporal comparison is different from those which are considered in the first sections of this chapter.

A comparison of welfare at two points in time t and t' is not based on a comparison of the utility derived from c_t and $c_{t'}$, but on the utility derived from the *infinite consumption streams* starting at t and t', respectively. Assume that $u(c_t, x_t)$ is actually an intertemporally comparable utility measure. In this case we may have

$$\int_{t_1}^\infty u(c_s, x_s)e^{-r(s-t)}ds > \int_{t_2}^\infty u(c_s, x_s)e^{-r(s-t)}ds$$

and simultaneously

$$u(c_{t_1}, x_{t_1}) < u(c_{t_2}, x_{t_2}).$$

According to the welfare concept in the tradition of Weitzman (1976), the welfare is in this case decreasing from t_1 to t_2, while with the welfare concept in the tradition of Nordhaus and Tobin (1972), the welfare would be increasing from t_1 to t_2. These two perspectives on intertemporal welfare comparison are thus different.

Returning to the question of intertemporal comparison using NWM, it should first be noted that both $\bar{H}_t$ and $u_c(c_t^*, x_t^*)$ in (6.4) will in general not be constant over time, and thus even when NWM is growing, H_t may be declining, and vice versa. To analyse this problem, we return to the linearization of the Hamiltonian. We avoid the problem that $\bar{H}_t$ and u_c change over time, if we ensure that we linearize H_t and $H_{t'}$ around the same point. We thus linearize $H_{t'}$ around the state at time t,

$$
\begin{aligned}
H_{t'} &= \qquad\qquad u(c_{t'}^*, x_{t'}^*) + p_{t'}^* \dot{k}_{t'}^* \\
&\approx \quad u(c_t^*, x_t^*) + u_c \cdot (c_{t'}^* - c_t^*) + u_x \cdot (x_{t'}^* - x_t^*) + p_{t'}^* \dot{k}_{t'}^*,
\end{aligned}
$$

where u_c and u_x both are marginal utilities at time t. With this linearization we see that

$$
\begin{aligned}
H_{t'} - H_t &\approx u_c(c_{t'}^* - c_t^*) + u_x(x_{t'}^* - x_t^*) + p_t^*(\dot{k}_{t'}^* - \dot{k}_t^*) + (p_{t'}^* - p_t^*)\dot{k}_{t'}^* \\
&= NMW_{t'} - NMW_t + (p_{t'}^* - p_t^*)\dot{k}_{t'}^*,
\end{aligned}
$$

where NMW at time t' is computed with the prices from time t, thus $NMW_{t'} - NMW_t$ is the real growth. However, the welfare changes include an additional term $(p_{t'}^* - p_t^*)\dot{k}_{t'}^*$.

Usually, the last term, reflecting price changes, is only a second-order effect, but in this model that is not true. The value of capital represents the welfare from the future consumption that this capital makes possible. A first-order effect on future consumption will thus be represented by the price of capital. Intertemporal comparison of utility should thus also account for changes in the value of capital. Therefore NWM does not measure changes in welfare over time correctly. For a further discussion, see Brekke (1994).

Finally, we remember from Chapter 4 that the model assumes a stationary technology. At a national level, terms of trade and interest rate are part of the nation's technology. To apply this model on a national level thus requires constant terms of trade and interest rates and that assumption is hardly reasonable (see Asheim, 1995).

To summarize: apart from the problems of measuring welfare, as pointed out in Chapter 5, the NWM faces a number of additional problems. The model does not justify comparisons of NWM over time or between countries. Moreover the application to national economies requires that interest rates and terms of trade are constant.

6.6   ENVIRONMENTAL QUALITY INDICATORS

The income measures considered above are rather incomplete since they reflect only the potential restoration costs and not the actual damages due to environmental degradation. I have further argued that we cannot measure welfare. The alternative then would be to measure the determinants of welfare, or the environmental primary goods. This is probably one reason why *environmental indicators* have been brought on to the agenda in many countries and international organizations.

There are many reasons for developing physical indicators for the state of the environment. We argued above that the primary objective for improving the informational basis for environmental policy is not to measure welfare. Rather, the primary objective should be to make sure that the relevant aspects of the policy, including the effect on the environment, are taken into account in the political decision process. Information on which to base judgements is obviously important for proponents of both procedural and end state justice. We also argued that environmental quality fits well into the concept of primary goods, as something anyone with a rational plan of life wants, whatever else he/she may want. Primary goods are measured in physical units.

Several countries and organizations have worked on developing environmental indicators. For a discussion of this work in OECD, ECE,

Table 6.1 Proposed indicator set

Environmental issue	Environmental quality indicator
Climate change	Radiative forcing
Ozone depletion	Total ozone column
Health	Person-episode days
Noise	Persons exposed to noise above threshold
Eutrophication	State of major lake
Acidification: forest	Crown density in forests
Acidification: fish	Lakes with damaged fish populations
Contamination	Eggshell thickness of predatory birds
Recreation	Access to wilderness areas
Biodiversity	Area of rare biotopes

Source: Alfsen and Sæbø (1993)

UNSO, Canada, Norway, Sweden and Denmark, see Alfsen and Sæbø (1993). The proposed indicators are usually directed towards decision makers and the general public, and intended to give an overview of the state of the environment. The number of indicators in the different proposals ranges from ten to fifty.

The indicators proposed in Alfsen and Sæbø (1993) (based on Alfsen et al., 1991) illustrate this approach. They suggest indicators for eight different areas. For each area a state of the environment indicator is chosen, and for seven of them they also suggest a stress indicator, indicating the external forces which contribute to changes in the state of the environment. The environmental quality indicators are the determinants of welfare, while the stress indicators are meant to show the forces behind these state indicators.

The proposed indicators are given in Table 6.1. Person-episode days are the number of persons exposed to pollution levels above guideline values, multiplied by the number of such conditions prevailing. Wilderness is defined as areas more than 5 km from roads. Note that this is an initial suggestion. Further work on this topic is carried out, for example in the OECD, whose proposal probably will be different from the one indicated in Table 6.1.

A brief look at the list shows that the use of physical indicators is not the answer to all our problems. The indicator for recreation measures only the availability of wilderness areas. These may be important recreation areas for some groups, but a large share of the population would rather use recreational areas that are easily accessible by road. Recreational services in the environment depend on the availability of beaches, areas of scenic beauty, wilderness areas, and so on. Since it is impossible to reflect this variety in one number, one is forced to choose a less than perfect measure.

Objections can be raised against almost any of the indicators. The thickness of an eggshell indicates contamination aggregated in the food chain. The indicator is mainly sensitive to DDT, and is not sensitive to other serious contamination problems. Person-episode days do not reflect the fact that episodes with pollution far above the threshold level are more dangerous than those just above the level, and that even episodes below the level may be dangerous in the long run.

Environmental quality is a rather complex issue, and even experts are struggling to understand the dynamic laws of ecological systems. We will have to accept that any limited set of indicators about the state of the environment must be a crude simplification of reality.

What a list of indicators such as the one above achieves, is to present a generally understandable and rather broad picture of the state of the environment. Whether environmental quality can be measured in monetary terms or not, such information will be important.

6.7 INCOME, WELFARE, OR ENVIRONMENTAL INDICATORS

There are at least three ways to account for environmental degradation. Either by extending the income measures to reflect restrictions on the degradation, or by developing welfare measures which include the welfare effects of environmental degradation or by seeing the environment as a primary good, and just recording the changes in physical terms. Within each of these approaches there are a variety of solutions. Income can be computed with different restrictions, welfare can represent instantaneous or discounted utility and the primary goods can be replaced by functionings to take different needs into account.

While I have argued that income can be corrected for the cost of restoring environmental degradation provided some restoration path has been determined, such adjustments will not represent the real importance of environmental changes. Welfare indicators would in principle give a comprehensive picture, provided national welfare is a well-defined and unique quantity that can be mesured. As I have argued in Chapter 5, I do not think that welfare is measurable. We are then left with the solution of providing environmental indicators, which will be imperfect, since a complex reality would have to be represented by a few numbers.

7. Conclusion

Are we depleting the world's natural resources at the expense of future generations? How should we best report the effects of resource extraction and changes in the natural environment which run alongside economic growth? Does the GDP growth in the industrialized world during last century really reflect the true changes in social welfare?

This book has addressed methodological issues related to these questions. Measurement of income can shed light on how much we can consume without leaving future generations poorer than ourselves, with the proviso that these measures are highly uncertain. On the question of comparing social welfare over time or between countries, I do not think there is only one possible answer. Social welfare should be discussed, not measured. Nevertheless, we need measures that give an overview of the things we need to know to hold an informed discussion about social welfare. There already exist a number of such indicators representing the economy, and similar indicators should be developed for the environment to ensure that environmental changes get the attention they deserve.

Let us briefly recapitulate the main argument concerning these three areas: income, social welfare and environmental indicators.

7.1 INCOME

We have interpreted Hicksian income as maximum sustainable consumption. If the interest rates are falling or the population is growing, then sustainability will require an increasing wealth. When population and interest rates are constant, keeping wealth constant is sufficient to be able to maintain the consumption level. In this case the Hicksian income is the return on wealth and the income from resource extraction will then be the return on resource wealth. This definition applies to any kind of natural resources.

We found that the income from the extraction of non–renewable resources will be positive and may even be higher than current resource rent. This conclusion is in contrast to Repetto et al. (1989), who claim that income in this case is zero unless new reserves are found, and El Serafy (1989) who claims that a percentage of the rent should count as income.

A fundamental problem with the measurement of income is future uncertainties. Calculations of income from petroleum extraction in Norway demonstrated that the uncertainties can be substantial. Under uncertainty, income was defined as the maximum a nation can consume subject to the constraint that expected future consumption should be at least as large as current consumption. Nevertheless, expected future consumption may be very different from actual future consumption. Therefore an important objective of future studies will be to account for the uncertainties in the definition of income.

The definition of income is not restricted to resource extraction, and may cover the entire national income. We argued that income can also partly reflect environmental issues, although only in a narrow sense. Given some path of restoration of environmental quality, we can compute the present value of the restoration cost. The return on this value should be deducted from the income.

This adjustment of income considers only the cost of restoration and ignores the benefits of improved environmental services. Furthermore, the method does not apply to damage which cannot be restored. Similarly if a damaged environmental site can be restored, but only in, say, 50 years, the welfare loss from that site during that time will not be counted. At the same time, income is very sensitive both to the sustainable standard and to the path along which it is reached. We would need to take the welfare consequences into account in choosing a restoration path in the first place. The adjustments of income for environmental degradation may be interesting, but they cannot replace other measures of the extent of environmental degradation.

7.2   WELFARE

A fundamental problem both with income measurement and with environmental indicators is the complexity of the information the indicator is meant to represent. At this point, welfare measures appear to offer an elegant solution since a social welfare function assigns one number to each social state, however complex. A welfare measure can also take into account environmental degradation without having to choose some arbitrary standard or assume that complete restoration is possible. On a pragmatic level, the complexity of the natural system would also be a challenge for a welfare measure, but from a theoretical point, the aggregation problem would be solved.

These advantages are soon lost if we have to accept that there is no unique ranking of social states, but that the ranking depends on who makes the judgement. Social welfare will then no longer be one index but a number of indexes. I have argued that since there is no objective method of measuring interpersonally comparable well-being, the ranking of social states will in fact depend on who makes the judgement.

To what extent these judgements will be different is an empirical question. If there is considerable degree of agreement on the welfare judgement, at least for some specific cases, then welfare indicators may provide a good solution to the many aggregation problems explicit and implicit in the discussion above.

I do not think that social welfare gives one objective ranking. I cannot see why everybody should make the same judgement about interpersonally comparable well-being. Nor do I share the welfaristic view that individual well-being is the only thing that matters for the ranking of social states. Moreover, preferences reflect such different plans of life that aggregating well-being seen as preference satisfaction does not make sense. From this perspective, social welfare is not something to measure, it is something we discuss.

Finally, we have identified two different approaches to the measurement of social welfare. One tradition, based on the work of Weitzman (1976) sees welfare as discounted utility, while the other tradition sees welfare as instantaneous utility. We have argued that the proposed measures of discounted utility are based on too restrictive an assumption to apply to small economies. Moreover, this welfare measure cannot be used for comparisons of welfare over time and between countries.

7.3 PRIMARY GOODS

Environmental indicators are a possible alternative to a welfare measure, and I have placed them under the heading of primary goods, to indicate the difference in the fundamental philosophy. It is possible, though, to take a more prosaic view on the difference.

Those who do not share my view on the possibility of measuring welfare may still find environmental indicators useful. Even for those who think that welfare is measurable, there will be many remaining issues to be clarified. Until these issues are resolved, we would need measures in physical units. Even with a welfare measure in place, we would need more detailed information to understand changes. Moreover, values are usually computed from quantities and prices. From this perspective the environmental indicators may be interesting supplementary quantitative information. For those who do not believe that welfare is a unique quantity, to be measured, information in physical units will be the only available solution.

Fortunately, the environment is too complex to be rated on a linear scale, but this poses a problem for the development of environmental indicators. It is an almost impossible task to represent the state of the environment by a few numbers. The task is not made easier if we add the restriction that each of these numbers should be easily understood by the general public.

We started this discussion with reference to the question of greening the GDP. Throughout the book, the focus has been on presenting the overall picture of the state of the nation. Inevitably, such a overall picture will have to ignore the richness and details of reality. That reality is richer than some national indicators can present, is not a pity. If we further accept that there is not a unanimous agreement on how to rank the different states of the nation, we will have to accept that no single number, not even a small set of numbers, can tell the whole truth about the development of a nation or how one nation compares with others.

Bibliography

Aaheim, A. and K. Nyborg (1995): 'On the interpretation and applicability of a green national product', *Review of Income and Wealth*, **41**, pp. 57–71.

Alfsen, K., T. Bye and L. Lorentsen (1986): *Natural Resource Accounting and Analysis, The Norwegian Experience*, Social and Economic Studies No 65, Statistics Norway, Oslo.

Alfsen, K. and H.V. Sæbø(1993): 'Environmental quality indicators, background, principles and examples from Norway', *Environmental and Resource Economics*, **3**, 415–35.

Alfsen, K., K.A. Brekke, F. Brunborg, K. Nyborg, H. Lurås and H.V. Sæbø(1991): 'Environmental Indicators', Discussion Paper No 71, Statistics Norway, Oslo.

Andreoni, J. (1990): 'Impure altruism and donations of public goods: A theory of warm-glow giving', *Economic Journal*, **100**, 464–77.

Arrow, J.K. (1951): *Social Choice and Individual Values*, New York: Wiley.

Arrow, J.K. (1977): 'Extended sympathy and the possibilities of social choice', *American Economic Review Papers and Proceedings*, 67, Reprinted in *Social Choice and Justice, Collected Papers of Kenneth J. Arrow*, Basil Blackwell, 1984, pp. 147–61.

163

Asheim, G.B. (1986): 'Hartwick's rule in open economies', *Canadian Journal of Economics*, **19**, 395–402 (Erratum, **20**, 177)

Asheim, G.B. (1994): 'Net national product as an indicator of sustainability', *Scandinavian Journal of Economics*, **96**, 257–65.

Asheim, G.B. (1995): 'Capital gains and net national product in open economies', *Journal of Public Economics*, **59**, 419–34.

Asheim G. B. and K.A. Brekke (1993): 'Sustainability when Resource Management has Stochastic Consequences', Discussion Paper No 86, Statistics Norway, Oslo.

Aslaksen, I., K.A. Brekke, T.A. Johnsen and A. Aaheim (1990): 'Petroleum resources and the management of national wealth', in Bjerkholt, Olsen and Vislie (eds) *Recent Modelling Approaches in Applied Energy Economics*, Chapman and Hall.

Aslaksen, I. and C. Koren (1995): 'The value of unpaid household work: Recent issues and estimation methods', Unpublished manuscript, Statistics Norway, Oslo.

Atkinson, A.B. and J. E. Stiglitz (1980): *Lectures in Public Economics*, Singapore: McGraw Hill.

Aukrust, O. (1994): 'The Scandinavian contribution to national accounting', in Z. Kenessey (ed.) *The Accounts of Nations*, Amsterdam: IOS Press, pp. 16–65.

Aune, J. and R. Lal (1994): 'The tropical soil productivity calculator – a model for assessing effects on soil management on productivity', in R. Lal and B.A. Stewards (eds) *Sustainable Management of Soil*, Chelsea, MI: Lewis Publishers.

Barber, W.J. (1967): *A History of Economic Thought*, London: Penguin Books.

Bartelmus, P. and J. van Tongeren (1994): 'Environmental Accounting: An Operational Perspective', Working Paper No 1, Department
for Economic and Social Information and Policy Analysis, United
Nations, New York.

Becker, G.S. (1976): *The Economic Approach to Human Behavior*,
Chicago: University of Chicago Press.

Bergman, L. (1990): 'General equilibrium effects of environmental policy: an AGE-modelling approach', Research paper No. 6415, Economic Research Institute, Stockholm School of Economics.

Bergson, A. (1938): 'A reformulation of certain aspects of welfare economics', *Quarterly Journal of Economics*, **52**, 314–44.

Berman, M. (1982): *All That is Solid Melts into Air: The Experience
of Modernity*, New York: Simon & Schuster

Bernheim, B.D. (1986): 'On the voluntary and involuntary provision of
public goods', *American Economic Review*, **76**, 789–93.

Braun, P.A., G.M. Constantinides and W.E. Ferson (1993): 'Time non-
separability in aggregate consumption: International and national
evidence', *European Economic Review*, **37**, 897–920.

Brekke, K.A. (1994): 'Net national product as a welfare measure', *Scandinavian Journal of Economics*, **96**, 241–52. .

Brekke, K.A. (1996): 'The numeraire matters in cost–benefit analysis',
forthcoming in *Journal of Public Economics*.

Brekke, K.A. and H.A. Gravningsmyhr (1994): 'Adjusting NNP for
Instrumental or Defensive Expenditures: An Analytical Approach',
Discussion Paper No. 134, Statistics Norway, Oslo.

Brekke, K.A., V. Iversen and J. Aune (1996): 'Soil Wealth in Tanzania',
Discussion Paper No 164, Statistics Norway, Oslo.

Brekke, K.A., H. Lurås and K. Nyborg (1994): 'Sufficient Welfare Indicators, Allowing for Disagreement in Evaluations of Social Welfare', *Journal of Economics*, **63**, 303–24.

Broome, J. (1993): 'A cause of preference is not an object of preference', *Social Choice and Welfare*, **10**, 57–68.

Buchanan, J.M. (1954): 'Social choice, democracy and free markets', *Journal of Political Economy*, **LXII**, 114–123.

Burrows, P. (1993): 'Patronising paternalism', *Oxford Economic Papers*, **45**, 542–74.

Bye, B., T. Bye and L. Lorentsen (1989): 'Studies of Industry, Environment and Energy Towards 2000', Discussion Paper No. 44, Statistics Norway, Oslo.

Conrad, K. and M. Schröeder (1990): 'The control of CO_2 emissions and its economic impact: an AGE model for a German state', Discussion Paper No. 421–90, Mannheim University.

Cornes, R. and T. Sandler (1994): 'The comparative static properties of the impure public goods model', *Journal of Public Economics*, **54**, 403–21.

Daly, H.E. (1991): 'Toward an environmental macroeconomics', *Land Economics*, **67**, 255-9

Daly, H.E. and J.B. Cobb (1990): *For the Common Good*, London: Green Print.

Dasgupta, P. (1990): 'The environment as a commodity', *Oxford Review of Economic Policy*, **6**, 51–67.

Dasgupta, P. and G.M. Heal (1979): *Economic Theory and Exhaustible Resources*, Cambridge: Cambridge University Press.

Devarajahn, S. and R.J. Weiner (1991): 'National Resource Depletion and National Income Accounting', unpublished note.

Diamond, P.A. and J.A. Hausman (1994): 'Contingent valuation: is some number better than no number?', *Journal of Economic Perspectives*, **8**, (4), 45–64.

Diewert, W.E. (1987): 'Index numbers', J. Eatwell, M. Milgate and P. Newman (eds), *The New Palgrave Dictionary of Economics*, Vol. 3 K–P, pp. 767–80.

Dittmar, H. (1992): *The Social Psychology of Material Possessions: To Have Is To Be*, Exeter: Harvester Wheatsheaf.

Dixit, A., P. Hammond and M. Hoel (1980): 'On Hartwick's rule for regular maximin paths of capital accumulation and resource depletion', *Review of Economic Studies*, **47**, 551–6.

Drèze, J. and A. Sen (1989): *Hunger and Public Action,* Oxford: Clarendon Press.

Drèze, J. and N.H. Stern (1987): 'The theory of cost benefit analysis', in A.J. Auerbach and M. Feldstein (eds), *Handbook of Public Economics*, Amsterdam: North-Holland, Vol. 2, pp. 909-89.

Dworkin, R. (1981): 'What is equality? Part 1: Equality of welfare' and 'What is equality? Part 2: Equality of resources', *Philosophy and Public Affairs*, **10**.

Easterlin, R.A. (1974): 'Does economic growth improve the human Lot', in David and Reder (eds), *Nations and Households in Economic Growth. Essays in Honor of Moses Abramovitz*, New York: Academic Press.

Edgeworth, F.Y. (1881): *Mathematical Physics*, London: C. Kegan Paul & Co.

Edmunds, J. and J. Reilly (1983): 'A long-term global energy–economic model of carbon dioxide release from fossil fuel use', *Energy Economics*, **5**, 74–88.

Eisner, R. (1988): 'Extended accounts for national income and product', *Journal of Economic Literature*, **26**, 1611–84.

El Serafy, S. (1989): 'The proper calculation of income from depletable natural resources', in Y.J. Ahmad, S. El Serafy and E. Lutz (eds), *Environmental Accounting for Sustainable Development*, Washington, DC: World Bank. pp 10–18.

Elster, J. (1986): 'The market as the forum: three varieties of political theory', in J. Elster and A. Hylland (eds), *Foundations of Social Choice Theory*, Cambridge: Cambridge University Press and Universitetsforlaget.

Elster, J. and J. Roemer (eds) (1992): *Interpersonal Comparison of Well-being*, Cambridge: Cambridge University Press.

Elwell, H. and M.A. Stockings (1982): 'Developing a simple yet practical method of soil-loss estimation', *Tropical Agriculture*, **59**, 43–8.

Farzin, Y.H. (1992): 'The time path of scarcity rent in the theory of exhaustible resources', *Economic Journal*, **102**, 813–30.

Fisher, I. (1930): *The Theory of Interest*, New York: Macmillan.

Flåm, S.D. (1993): 'Norsk sildeformue' (The Norwegian herring wealth), Notat 88, SEFOS.

Førsund, F.R. (1985): 'Input–output models, national economic models, and the environment', in A.V. Kneese and J.L. Sweeney (eds), *Handbook of Natural Resource and Energy Economics*, Vol. I, Amsterdam: North-Holland.

Førsund, F.R. and S. Strøm (1976): 'The generation of residual flows in Norway: an input–output approach', *Journal of Environmental Economics and Management*, **3**, 129–41.

Frank, R.H. (1985a): *Choosing the Right Pond*, NewYork: Oxford University Press.

Frank, R.H. (1985b): 'The demand for unobservable and other nonpositional goods', *American Economic Review*, **75**, 101–16.

Frank, R.H. (1992): 'Melding sociology and economics: James Coleman's foundations of social theory', *Journal of Economic Literature*, **XXX**, 147–70.

Frisch, R. (1939): (Comments on a paper by Erik Lindahl) 'I: Beretning om Det 3. nordiske statistikermøte i Oslo den 28. og 29. juni 1939.' (Reports from the 3rd meeting of nordic statisticians in Oslo, 28-29 July, 1939), in Norwegian.

Glomsrød, S., H. Vennemo and T. Johnsen (1992): 'Stabilization of emissions of CO_2, a computable general equilibrium assessment', *Scandinavian Journal of Economics*, **94**, 53–69.

Graaff, J. de V. (1957): *Theoretical Welfare Economics*, Cambridge: Cambridge University Press.

Gray, L.C. (1914): 'Rent under the assumption of exhaustibility', *Quarterly Journal of Economics*, **28**, 466–89.

Grossman, G.M. (1995): 'Pollution and growth: what do we know?', in I. Goldin and L.A. Winters (eds.), *The Economics of Sustainable Development*, Cambridge: Cambridge University Press.

Hahneman, M. (1994): 'Valuing the environment through contingent valuation', *Journal of Economic Perspectives*, **8**, (4), 19–44.

Hall, D.C. and J.V. Hall (1984): 'Concepts and measures of natural resource scarcity with a summary of recent trends', *Journal of Environmental Economics and Management*, **11**, 363–79.

Hanesson, R. (1991): 'En samfunnsøkonomisk lønnsom fiskenæring. Struktur, gevinst, forvaltning' (An efficient fishery sector: Structure, benefits, management.) in Norwegian, Arbeidsnotat No. 21, SNF-Bergen.

Hanley, N. and C.L. Spash (1993): *Cost–Benefit Analysis and the Environment*, Aldershot: Edward Elgar.

Hareide, D. (1991): *Det gode Norge; På vei mot et med mennsekelig samfunn?* (The good Norway: towards a humane society?), in Norwegian, Oslo: Gyldendal.

Harsanyi, J. (1955): 'Cardinal welfare, individual ethics and interpersonal comparison', *Journal of Political Economy*, **63**, 309–21.

Harsanyi, J. (1987): 'Von Neumann–Morgenstern utilities, risk taking and welfare', in G.R. Feiwel (eds), *Arrow and the Ascent of Modern Economic Theory*, London: Macmillan. pp. 545-58.

Hartwick, J. (1977): 'Intergenerational equity and the investing of rents from exhaustible resources', *American Economic Review*, **67**, 972–74.

Hartwick, J. (1990): 'Natural resources, national accounting and economic depreciation', *Journal of Public Economics*, **43**, 291–304.

Hartwick, J. and A. Hageman (1993): 'Economic depreciation of mineral stocks and the contribution of El Serafy,' in E. Lutz (ed.), pp 211-35.

Hausman, D.M. and M.S. McPherson (1996): *Economic Analysis and Moral Philosophy*, Cambridge: Cambridge University Press.

Hicks, J. (1939): 'The foundation of welfare economics', *Economic Journal*, **49**, 696–700, 711–12.

Hicks, J. (1940): 'The valuation of the social income', *Economica*, **VII**, 105–24.

Hicks, J. (1946): *Value and Capital*, 2nd edn, Oxford: Oxford University Press.

Hicks, J. (1965): *Capital and Growth*, Reprinted as an appendix in Hicks, 1985, *Methods of Dynamic Economics*, Oxford: Clarendon Press.

Hirsch, F. (1976): *Social Limits to Growth*, Cambridge, MA: Harvard University Press.

Hotelling, H. (1931): 'The economics of exhaustible resources', *Journal of Political Economy*, **39**, 137–75.

Houghton, J.T., B.A. Callander and J. Ephraums (eds) (1990): *Climate Change – The IPCC Scientific Assessment*, WMO, UNEP, IPCC, Cambridge: Cambridge University Press.

Hueting, R. (1989): 'Correcting national income for environmental losses: toward a practical solution', In Y.J. Ahmad, S. El Serafy and E. Lutz (eds), *Environmental Accounting for Sustainable Development*, Washington, DC: World Bank. pp 32–9

Hueting, R., P. Bosh and B. de Boer (1992): 'Methodology for the Calculation of Sustainable National Income', Statistical Essays M44, Statistics Netherland.

IEA (International Energy Agency) (1987): *Energy Conservation in IEA Countries*, Paris: OECD.

Jaszi, G. (1973): Comment, in M. Moss (eds), *The Measurement of Economic and Social Performance*, New York: Colombia University Press.

Johansson, P.O. (1992): 'Altruism in cost–benefit analysis', *Environmental and Resource Economics*, **2**, 605–13.

Johansson, P.O. (1994): 'Altruism and the value of statistical life: empirical implications', *Journal of Health Economics*, **13**, 111–18.

Jorgenson, D.W. (1993): 'Aggregate consumer behaviour and the measurement of social welfare', *Econometrica*, **58**, 1007–40.

Jorgenson, D.W. and P.J. Wilcoxen (1993): 'Reducing US carbon dioxide emissions: An assessment of different instruments', *Journal of Policy Modeling*, **15**, 495–520.

Kahneman, D. and J. Knetch (1992) 'Valuing public goods: the purchase of moral satisfaction', *Journal of Environmental Economics and Management*, **22**, 57–70.

Kahneman, D. and C. Varey (1992): 'Notes on the psychology of utility' in J. Elster and J. Roemer (eds), pp 127–63.

Kaldor, N. (1939): 'Welfare proposition of economics and interpersonal comparison of utility', *Economic Journal*, **49**, 549–51.

Kemp, M.C. and Y.-K. Ng (1976): 'On the existence of social welfare functions: social orderings and social decision functions', *Economica*, **43**, 59–66.

Keuning, S.J. (1993): 'An information system for environmental indicators in relation to the national accounts', in W.F.M. de Vries, G.P. den Bakker, M.B.G. Gircour, S.J. Keuning and A. Lenson (eds), *The Value Added ofNational Accounting*, pp. 287–305.

Kjelby, T. (1993): 'De norske torskefiskeriene som nasjonalformue' (The Norwegian cod fisheries as national wealth) in Norwegian, Notat 90, SEFOS, Bergen.

Kreps, D. (1989): *A Course in Microeconomic Theory*, Princeton, NJ: Princeton University Press.

Listhaug, O. and B. Huseby (1990): 'Value in Norway: Study Description and Codebook', ISS-report No. 11, Department of Sociology, University of Trondheim.

Lucas R.E. Jr. (1988): 'On the mechanics of economic development', *Journal of Monetary Economics*, **22**, 3–42.

Lutz, E. (ed.) (1993): *Toward Improved Accounting for the Environment*, Washington, DC: World Bank.

Mäler, K,-G. (1991): 'National accounts and environmental resources', *Environment and Resource Economics*, **1**, 1–15.

Manne, A.S. and R.G. Richels (1990): 'CO_2 emission limits: An economic cost analysis for the USA', *Energy Journal*, **11**, 87–108.

Manne, A.S. and L. Schrattenholzer (1988): *International Energy Workshop, Overview of Poll Response and Frequency Distribution*, Laxemburg, Austria: IIASA.

Milgrom, P. (1993): 'Is sympathy an economic value? Philosophy, economics and the contingent valuation', in J.A. Hausman (ed.), *Contingent Valuation: A Critical Assessment*, New York: North-Holland.

Mitchell, R.C. and R.T. Carsson (1989): *Using Surveys to Value Public Goods*, Washington: Resources for the Future.

Moum, K. (ed.) (1992): *Klima, økonomi og tiltak – KLØKT* (Climate, economy and policy), Report No. 3, Statistics Norway, Oslo.

Mueller, D.C. (1989): *Public Choice II*, Cambridge: Cambridge University Press.

Nordhaus, W.O. (1992): 'Lethal Model 2: The Limits to Growth Revisited' *Brookings Paper on Economic Activity*, **2**, 1–59.

Nordhaus, W. and J. Tobin (1972): *Is Growth Obsolete?*, National Bureau of Economic Research, General Series 96.

Nozik, R. (1974): *Anarchy, State, and Utopia*, New York: Basic Books.

Ohlsson, I. (1953): *On National Accounting*, Stockholm: Konjunkturinstitutet.

Olsson, M. (1965): *The Logic of Collective Action*, Cambridge, MA: Harvard University Press.

Page, T. (1983): 'Intergenerational justice as opportunity', in MacLean and Brown (eds), *Energy and the Future*, Totowa, NJ: Rowman & Littlefield..

Parks, R.P. (1976): 'An impossibility theorem for fixed preferences: a dictatorial Bergson–Samuelson welfare function', *Review of Economic Studies*, **43**, 447–50.

Pearce, D.W. and G. Atkinson (1995): 'Measuring sustainable development', in D. Bromley (ed.), *The Handbook of Environmental Economics*, Cambridge, UK: Blackwell.

Pearce, D.W., E.B. Barbier and A. Markandya (1990): *Sustainable Development*, London: Earthscan.

Pearce,D.W. and J.J. Warford (1993): *World Without End*, Washington DC: Oxford University Press.

Peskin, H.M. (1996): 'Alternative Resource and Environmental Accounting Concepts and their Contribution to Policy', Paper presented at the IARIW conference, Tokyo, 5–8 March.

Pezzey, J. (1992): 'Sustainability: an interdisciplinary guide,' *Environmental Values*, **1**, 321–62.

Pigou, A. (1920): *Economics of Welfare*, London: Macmillan

Pollak, R. (1991): 'Welfare comparisons and situation comparisons', *Journal of Econometrics*, **50**, 31–48.

Portney, P.R. (1994): 'The contingent valuation debate: why should economists care?', *Journal of Economic Perspectives*, **8**, (4), 3–18.

Postel, S. (1990): 'Towards a new "eco"-nomics', *World Watch*, September–October, 20–28.

Randall, A. and M.C. Farmer (1995): 'Benefits, cost, and the safe minimum standard of conservation', in D. Bromley (ed.), *Handbook of Environmental Economics*, Cambridge UK: Blackwell.

Rawls, J. (1971): *A Theory of Justice*, Oxford: Oxford University Press.

Repetto, R, W. Magrath, M. Wells, C. Beer and F. Rossini (1989): *Wasting Assets: Natural Resources in the National Income Accounts*, World Resource Institute.

Ruggles, N.D. (1987): 'Social accounting', in J. Eatwell, M. Milgate and P. Newman (eds), *The New Palgrave Dictionary of Economics*, Vol. 4: Q–Z, pp. 377–82.

Rutherford, T. (1992): 'The welfare effect of fossil carbon restrictions: results from a recursively dynamic trade model', OECD Economic Department Working Paper No. 112, Paris.

Ryder H. and G. Heal (1973): 'Optimal growth with intertemporally dependent preferences', *Review of Economics Studies*, **40**, 1–33.

Sagoff, M. (1988): *The Economy of the Earth*, Cambridge: Cambridge University Press.

Samuelson, P.A. (1947): *Foundation of Economic Analysis*, Cambridge, MA: Harvard University Press.

Samuelson, P.A. (1977): 'Reaffirming the existence of "Reasonable" Bergson–Samuelson social welfare functions', *Economica*, **44**, 81–8.

Scitovsky, T. (1976): *The Joyless Economy*, New York: Oxford University Press.

Sefton, J.A. and M.R. Weale (1996): 'The net national product and exhaustible resources: the effect of foreign trade', *Journal of Public Economics*, **61**, 21–47.

Sen, A.K. (1970): *Collective Choice and Social Welfare*, San Francisco: Holden Day.

Sen, A. K. (1976a): 'Real national income', *Review of Economic Studies*, **43**, 19–39.

Sen, A.K. (1976b): 'Welfare inequalities and Rawlsian axiomatics', *Theory and Decision*, **7**, 243–62. Reprinted in R. Butts and J. Hinitikka (1977), *Fundamental Problems in the Special Sciences*, Dortrecht: D. Reidel.

Sen, A.K. (1979): 'Personal utilities and public judgements: or What's wrong with welfare economics?', *Economic Journal*, **89**, 537–58.

Sen, A.K. (1983): 'Poor, relatively speaking', *Oxford Economic Papers*, **35**, 153-69.

Sen, A.K. (1985a): *Commodities and Capabilities*, Amsterdam: North-Holland.

Sen, A.K. (1985b): 'Well-Being, Agency and freedom: the Dewey Lecture 1984', *Journal of Philosophy*, **LXXXII**, 169–221.

Sen, A.K. (1986): 'Social choice theory', in K.J. Arrow and M.D. Intrilligator (eds), *Handbook of Mathematical Economics*, Vol. III, Amsterdam: North-Holland, pp. 1075–181.

Sen, A.K. (1991) 'Welfare, preference and freedom', *Journal of Econometrics*, **50**, 15–29.

Sen, A.K. (1993): 'The economics of life and death', *Scientific American*, May, 18–25.

Sen, A.K. and B. Williams (1982): *Utilitarianism and Beyond*, Cambridge: Cambridge University Press.

Sennet, R. (1990): *The Conscience of the Eye: The Design and Social Life of Cities*, New York: Knopf.

Slade, M.E. (1982): 'Trends in natural-resource commodity prices: an analysis of the time domain', *Journal of Environmental Economics and Management*, **9**, 122–37.

Smith, V.K. (1993): 'Comment: Arbitrary values, good causes and premature verdicts', *Journal of Environmental Economics and Management*, **22**, 71–89.

Smullyan, (1980): *This Book Needs No Title*, Englewood Cliffs, NJ: Prentice Hall, p. 56.

SNA (System of National Account) (1993), Commission for the European Communities, International Monetary Fund, Organization for Economic Cooperation and Development, United Nations, World Bank, Brussel/Luxembourg, New York, Paris, Washington, DC.

Solow, R.M. (1986): 'On the intergenerational allocation of natural resources', *Scandinavian Journal of Economics*, **88**, 141–9.

Solow, R.M. (1993): 'Sustainability: an economist's perspective', in R. Dorfman and N. Dorfman (eds), *Economics of the Environment*, 3rd edition, New York: Norton.

Stark, O. (1991): *The Migration of Labor*, Cambridge, MA: Blackwell.

Starrett, D. (1988): *Foundations of Public Economics*, Cambridge: Cambridge University Press.

Statistics Norway (1993): *Social Outlook 1993*, Oslo.

Statistics Norway (1995): *Natural Resources and the Environment 1995*, Oslo.

Stigum, B. (1990): *Toward a Formal Science of Economics*, Cambridge, MA: MIT Press.

Stoorvogel, J.J. and E. M.A. Smaling (1990): 'Assessment of soil nutrient depletion in Sub-Saharan Africa: 1983–2000', Report 28, Winard Staring Center, Wageningen, Holland.

Strand, J. (1985): 'Verdsetting av reduserte luftforurensinger fra biler i Norge' (Valuing reduced pollution from automobiles in Norway.) in Norwegian, Memorandum No. 1, Department of Economics, University of Oslo.

Sugden, R. (1984): 'Reciprocity: the supply of public goods through voluntary contribution', *Economic Journal*, **94**, 772–84.

Sugden, R. (1993): 'Welfare, resources, and capabilities: a review of *Inequality Reexamined* by Amartya Sen', *Journal of Economic Literature*, **XXXI**, 1947–62.

Svensson, L.E.O. (1986). "Comments on Solow: on the intergenerational allocation of natural resources', *Scandinavian Journal of Economics*, **88**, 153–5.

Tinbergen, J. (1991): 'On the measurement of welfare', *Journal of Econometrics*, **50**, 7–13.

United Nations (1993): *Integrated Environmental and Economic Accounting: Interim version*, New York: United Nations.

UNDP (United Nations Development Programme) (1993): *World Development Report 1993*, Oxford University Press, New York: UNDP

Usher, D. (1994): 'Income and the Hamiltonian', *Review of Income and Wealth*, **40**, 123–41.

von Neumann, J. and O. Morgenstern (1944): *Theory of Games and Economic Behaviour*, Princeton, NJ: Princeton University Press (2nd edn 1947; 3rd edn 1953).

WCED (World Commission on Environment and Development) (1987): *Our Common Future*, Oxford: Oxford University Press.

Weitzman, M. (1976): 'On the welfare significance of national product in the dynamic economy', *Quarterly Journal of Economics*, **90**, 156–62.

Weymark, J.A. (1992): 'A reconsideration of the Harsanyi–Sen debate on utilitarianism', in Elster and Roemer (eds), pp. 255-320.

World Bank (1986): *World Development Report 1986*, New York: Oxford University Press.

WRI (World Resource Institute) (1986): *World Resources 1986*, New York: Oxford University Press.

WRI (World Resource Institute) (1994): *World Resources 1994–95*, New York: Oxford University Press.

Index